CRY GOD FOR ENGLAND

Cry GOD for England

The Survival and Mission of the British Churches

JAMES BENTLEY

THE BOWERDEAN PRESS · 1978

First published in 1978 by
The Bowerdean Press
15 Blackfriars Lane
London EC4V 6ER

© Copyright 1978 James Bentley

Designed by Douglas Martin
Photoset, printed and bound in Great Britain by
Redwood Burn Limited, Trowbridge and Esher.

British Library Cataloguing in Publication Data

Bentley, James
    Cry God for England.
    1. Great Britain – Church history – 20th century
    I. Title
    274.1   BR759

ISBN 0–906097–05–3
ISBN 0–906097–06–1   Pbk

Contents

*For Joanna and Emma
with love and prayers*

Preface

This book is a substantially rewritten version of six documentary programmes which I presented on B.B.C. radio, investigating the health and future prospects of the British churches. Wherever I quote a person without a reference, the source is an interview made in preparing these programmes. My first thanks must therefore be to Mrs Wendy Maughan and Mrs Marilyn Barnes, who spent many laborious hours transcribing tape-recordings.

My debt is obvious to all those who gave up their time to talk to me. They are listed in the section *Who's Who* at the end of the book, but I thank them here (without in any way implying that they agree with all I have to say).

The Revd Michael Mayne made many fruitful suggestions at the time of the broadcasts. As well as providing information acknowledged in the text, Dr Stuart Mews delighted me by drawing attention to the report in the *Methodist Recorder* used in chapter 2. I am grateful for the help I was given by Professor R. S. Barbour, Miss Helen Morrice, the Revd Harry Undy, Miss Barbara Vellacott and Mrs Antoinette Wye. For incidental acts of kindness, I should like to thank Dr Bryan Wilson who showed me round the Codrington Library, Professor David Martin who made coffee that I could not drink (because I discovered that the clocks in the London School of Economics were wrong and I was about to miss my train), and Archbishop Derek Worlock who mended my tape-recorder.

Above all I wish to thank the Revd Leslie Mitchell not only for suggesting that I make the broadcasts (which he produced), but also for the very many profitable hours I spent with him as we travelled Britain in search of the Kingdom.

JAMES BENTLEY
June 1978

Except a grain of wheat fall into the ground
and die, it abides by itself alone; but
if it die, it bears much fruit

John 12.24

[1]
Crisis, or Turning-Point

'Most vicars do not really think', Jill Tweedie told me, apparently forgetting that she was talking to one. As a perceptive and responsible journalist she admits that Christians still devote themselves individually to countless good works; but she believes they have lost touch with the main issues of life because, she alleges, in church 'you are actually encouraged not to use your brain'.

Jill Tweedie attributes this to what she describes as 'the essence of religion itself: the suspension of thought' – a phrase I find reminiscent of the atheism considered *avant garde* in the years before World War I. It is today perfectly possible to accept the Christian faith without lapsing into immaturity, suspending thought or sacrificing logic.[1] Indeed there is evidence that the intellectual standing of Christianity is now far greater among thoughtful people than it was at the beginning of the twentieth century.[2]

Yet at one alarming point Jill Tweedie's observation about vicars may well be correct. At the beginning of the 1960s an exhaustive survey commissioned by the Church of England discovered that the inflexibility of the parochial system was not only impeding the exercise of the Church's pastoral ministry; it was also producing despair among the clergy. One incumbent, typical of many, felt 'a sense of being held fast in a machine that grinds endlessly on.'[3] Trapped in an outdated pattern of ministry, such men were finding it easier not to think about the strategy or effectiveness of their work. A few years later a Christian sociologist noted that clergymen in general, not simply Anglicans, were disinclined to confront the reality of social change. They preferred psychoanalytic or existential models of the world, which seemed to threaten them less. 'Unfortunately,' the sociologist commented, 'clergy are not able to live in the fantasy world of the well-heeled therapist: they must come to grips with structures eventually.'[4]

In such a situation the Churches inevitably began to function increasingly badly. One observer, shortly to become a Christian, described their performance as hilarious. The Church of England, he wrote, had long been the subject of derision. Its lovely buildings were falling into decay, and its clergy were for the most part forlorn and negligible. He believed the Dissenters were already finished; and to his surprise he found the Roman Catholics embarking on the same disastrous road. The Churches, he concluded, were in a state of shambles.[5]

The most obvious evidence of sociological change and cause of clerical malaise was a steep decline in the number of persons attending church. Of course such expansion or decline can be seen properly in perspective only over a period of centuries.[6] For example, Dr Edward Norman instances the very large decline in attendance at the Established Church in the second half of the eighteenth century as evidence of the failure of agricultural labourers to go to church.[7] Yet in the first half of the next century, in spite of the breakdown of the parochial structure in the cities, English institutional Christianity began to flourish again. According to the religious census of 1851, out of a total population of nearly 18 millions 3,773,474 persons attended the Church of England and 3,487,558 attended Roman Catholic and nonconformist churches on one Sunday. But in spite of the massive efforts of Victorian churchmen the number of worshippers once again began to decline.

This decline has continued to the present day. Already in the 1960s it had become a cause for serious concern.[8] Now the position is worse. The Church of England confirmed 157,000 persons in 1964 and only 96,000 ten years later — a drop of over 38 per cent. The Roman Catholic Church confirmed 90,000 in 1964 and only 70,000 ten years later. And the membership of the Methodist Church fell by 34,000 in the two years between 1968 and 1970.[9] Fewer men offer themselves for the sacred ministry. Fewer persons are baptised or marry in church. Dr Bryan

Wilson, reader in sociology in the University of Oxford, sums up the situation of the Churches today as 'a very considerable institutional presence – the buildings, the hierarchy of the church itself, the assemblies of the Free Churches, their conferences – but without a real solid base among the general public.'

The decline covers the whole of traditional Christendom and is apparently accelerating. But there are exceptions. David Martin, professor of sociology at the London School of Economics, points out that it does not apply to the small sects, the Jehovah's Witnesses and the Mormons and some of the varieties of what he calls 'religious fringe medicine'. Instead there has been a strengthening of the rather close in-group. Professor Martin adds that 'the ones that have suffered most are those forms of Protestant semi-rationalised Christianity that were the mainstream of Free Church belief and practice in England.'

According to David Martin the strength of Roman Catholics varies from country to country. Compared to what the Catholic Church has suffered in Holland, France, Italy and even America, he judges that in Britain it has undergone 'quite moderate attrition'. Professor Martin believes that this attrition is not simply the result of sociological forces over which the Church has no control. Partly it is the result of the reforms set in motion at the second Vatican Council, reforms like the Mass in English, co-operation with other Churches, a new insistence on religious liberty, which have seriously disorganised Roman Catholics. These reforms, however desirable and necessary they may have been, are creating problems of authority in a Church whose authority seemed not only part of its essential nature but also a most attractive part. As John Henry Newman wrote in the year of his conversion to Roman Catholicism, 'we yield to the authority of the Church in the questions and developments of faith,' principally because 'some authority there must be if there is a revelation, and other authority there is none but she.'[10] The questioning of that authority has reached such a pitch that a former professor at the Pontifical Biblical Institute in Rome has predicted that 'Well before the year 2000, there will no longer be a religious institution recognizable as the

Roman Catholic and Apostolic Church of today.'[11]

Since problems of authority are involved in the way all our Churches regard their lay members, they are not confined to Roman Catholicism. The issue is discussed in greater detail later in this book. Here it is simply set, alongside 'the irrationality and ineffectiveness of the present working arrangements of the Church of England'[12] (and, I think of other Churches too), as another reason why the institutional Churches are losing their members.

Such reasons lie within the control of Christians; but a deeper cause of decline in lay support for Christianity could lie outside their control: the general process of secularisation in our society. Secularisation is an emotive word.[13] Indeed, Professor David Martin believes it should be 'erased from the sociological dictionary', since it is 'less a scientific concept than a tool of counter-religious ideologies.'[14] Yet in spite of the possibilities of ideological distortion sociologists and historians have continued to find the concept useful in explaining the development of the present-day situation. Bryan Wilson sees secularisation as involving a tendency for the ordinary person less and less to consider any supernatural element with respect to his own daily life. 'He does not think, "Now that I'm to do this, what would God think about it?" or "What is the will of God as far as my marriage, my mortgage, the education of my children is concerned?" or whatever else it may be that he is doing.' As a result, what the Churches have to say or preach, and what happens in church services, become less and less relevant to him.

This has not happened overnight. Professor Owen Chadwick's analysis of marriage statistics in Britain from 1844 to 1904 leads him to the conclusion that 'through the Victorian age England grew much more secular.'[15] The point has now been reached where Christianity seems irrelevant to many of the main concerns of life. As a result Bryan Wilson believes that 'religious activity will become more and more manifestly a leisure activity, an expression of purely personal, almost idiosyncratic interests, which others will simply tolerate.'

Not only might Christians quail at the difficulties of trying to reverse such a trend; they also are subject to the danger of giving in to it, of accepting a marginal role in society. Jill Tweedie maintains that the Churches have developed a genius for fighting on the most irrelevant issues. Whenever the Churches come to her attention, she says, she is angered by the way they seem to pick on what she calls 'the absolutely most unimportant issues of our time'. Jill Tweedie instances the Churches' condemnation of a Danish film-maker who in 1976 and 1977 tried to make a film in Britain about the supposed sex-life of Jesus Christ. 'To think,'she says, 'that the Churches (and indeed the Prime Minister and the Queen for that matter) can get involved in something so absolutely irrelevant to anything that is truly important today is horrifying.'

As Jill Tweedie rightly asserts, there are at this time issues like poverty and torture that are more important than pornographic films about Jesus. Yet for my part I think Christians are perfectly justified in condemning such films, provided they do not forget the other issues. Christians ought to be concerned not only with the public presentation of the image of Jesus but also with the effects of pornography in general. Nevertheless, whilst disagreeeing with Jill Tweedie's example of our alleged irrelevance I find it bracing when someone in her position grows angry because we seem to be putting our energies behind the wrong causes. In so far as the weakness of the Churches today arises out of our obtuseness in seeing what matters, or even our wilful stupidity, something might be done about it.

Many in the Churches would claim they are already trying to do something about increasing our relevance. They have made changes and tried to come to terms with the twentieth century. The most dramatic changes have been made in Roman Catholicism as a result of the second Vatican Council; but wherever one looks in the other Churches also one sees new patterns of worship, new forms of ministry, women priests fully or partially accepted, and so on.

Bryan Wilson maintains that such changes can make little difference to our plight; to him they are merely 'tinkering around with the externals' and do not alter the fundamental fact that the Churches' values appear to be less and less determinant for relationships in the modern world. 'The fact that the Churches cannot make alterations to their values' is pinpointed by Dr Wilson as 'the crucial dilemma' for Christians. 'On the other hand,' he adds, 'if they did make alterations to that message, that fundamental message of man's humanness to man, then I don't know what good there would be in the Church either. So I think they are in a very difficult position and I don't see a way out of it.'

Now as a theologian I would want to disagree very strongly with Bryan Wilson here. The essence of Christianity is not a message at all, defined as 'man's humanness to man' or in any other way. It is not an idea or an attitude, but a person, Jesus Christ, whom the Churches exist to worship and commend to others. This comes before all questions of value or dogma. As Paul Althaus expressed it, in a famous phrase: 'I know not whether I believe; but I do know in whom I believe.'[16] Christians aproach and explore new aspects of their personal, social and political life in the light of Jesus Christ and the Churches' thinking about him. So Karl Barth at the very end of his life could declare: 'The last word which I have to say as a theologian and also as politician is not a term like "grace", but a name, "Jesus Christ".'[17]

In consequence Christians do not rely solely on time-honoured values. As their traditions about Jesus Christ meet new situations and problems, they expect new insights. As a result of this process the Christian message is developed and even changed.

Yet Bryan Wilson's warning cannot be entirely ignored. However Christianity seeks to cope with secularisation, it will be disastrous to do so by capitulating to it. Many aspects of present-day society are basically hostile to Christianity. If, as I shall argue, we need many more clergymen working outside the traditional church structures, 'in the world' so to speak, they must not accommodate themselves to the secular on its own terms. So there is a paradox: Jill Tweedie asks why the Churches remain irrelevant instead of bringing themselves up to date and concerning themselves with the real issues of today; whereas the sociologists suggest that by going along with current trends, far from making ourselves relevant, we may lose altogether any distinctive Christian reality. In desperately pursuing the modern age to the extent that we cease to be rooted in what is fundamental to Christianity, we shall loose our own strength.

Tinkering around with externals instead of facing the present age in the light of our great traditions is equally likely to weaken the Churches. Professor David Martin is quite specific about some of the ways in which we are making this kind of error. The great symbols of fatherhood and brotherhood and of fire (especially the 'fire-next-time', the notion that if we cut ourselves off from God and our fellow-men we are doomed to some kind of Hell), these symbols David Martin calls the Churches' most fundamental asset. The Churches themselves were almost creatures of such huge collective myths and symbols, to which people were able to relate and which the Churches expressed. Now they have been virtually eradicated from Christian thinking and liturgy. To the extent that the Church has smoothed out its language, 'made its language roughly the same as the language of the man in the office', as David Martin puts it, the Church has actually cut off the sources of its own vitality.

So I think the Churches are in deep trouble, partly of their own making and partly not. Stupidly we have progressively impoverished ourselves, cutting ourselves off from the fundamental symbols of the faith which might still relate to things that matter in people's lives. We have cut ourselves off too from the powerful and traditional language of our worship and sacred writings that once was capable of expressing people's deepest needs.

At the same time the Churches are caught in a situation over which we have no control. How can we reverse the process of our civilisation and put the clock back to a time when our values and our institutions really seemed to belong to society? The dilemma is this: twentieth century society apparently turns its back on what we have to offer; but the moment we abandon what we have to offer in order to catch up with society, we find we have abandoned something essential to our existence.

For these reasons the Churches are reaching crisis-point. At the same time it must be emphasised that our problems cannot be understood in isolation. They make sense only in a wider context, for what is happening to us is happening to many other organisations too. David Martin detects a general apathy towards all active ordinary voluntary association in Britain today. Trade Union meetings and political meetings as well as religious services are all under considerable pressure.[18] 'The situation of the mainstream Churches,' he says, 'the ordinary high street Churches, is part of the way in which the middle-of-the-road, that ordinary, rational, fairly commonsensical, not over-ethusiastic centre, is being pushed aside.' The Churches were one part of that centre.

Professor Martin draws attention secondly to a change in the style whereby people today try to persuade us that something or other is true. The old style of the Churches – sermons, reading, meditation, thinking together – is being replaced by the style of television which, in David Martin's words, 'creeps up on you in your parlour, which smooches up on you and which doesn't state its position directly. It basically whispers in your ear, as a private person in your home.' That style is very different from the old pattern of coming together in a public place and evaluating what a man has to say. The Churches are suffering from that change.

As a Christian himself, David Martin makes no secret of the fact that he deplores some of these developments. He also points out that some theorists today hold that any kind of public institution or structure, be it a church or a school, destroys the right of the individual to do his own thing. They believe that any kind of coming together, as for example in a school assembly, hampers people's individual impulses. Schools are built without any hall in which members can come together and develop a sense of *esprit de corps*. The mistaken theory is that we can gather either religious or educational experience by wandering where we will. David Martin describes this as a profound mistake. 'All that happens,' he says, 'is in fact disintegration.' At the same time he believes that today we are setting up structures so large and impersonal and bureaucratic that no-one can relate to them. They contain no fundamental symbolism with which people can connect.

I believe that instead of trying to counteract some of these tendencies the Churches themselves have set up similar impersonal and bureaucratic structures. But before asking how matters might begin to be put right, I have one prior question: how new is this situation? In some ways the Churches have been in trouble for a very long time. Dr Edward Norman, Dean of Peterhouse College, Cambridge, put it in an historical perspective. 'The one thing I do try to learn from the past in my own work as an historian,' he said, 'is that everything is extremely relative and that in every generation people will make their own mistakes; but they will be mistakes that are made in every generation by others in another way.' If that is the case, inevitably we in the Churches today will get some of the answers wrong. We need not be too anxious, even when people like Jill Tweedie grow angry with us.

Since, as Edward Norman spells out, each generation throws up its own corruptions of the faith, its own misunderstandings, its own failure to attend to its duties – ours probably no more than any other – there is a danger in looking back to a supposed golden age of religion. Edward Norman refuses to be over-impressed by social facts about the present religious scene. He points out that throughout the nineteenth century church leaders were constantly oppressed by a sense of crisis, believing that the social conditions of their age were inimical to religion and that social facts were stacked against religious faith being seen as true and spreading. Dr Norman's judgement is that 'we now look back and see a great age of faith, because educated opinion looked to Christianity to be the way in which the best that society could offer would be expressed.'

There, however, lies a difference between the nineteenth century and our own age. People are not looking for this to the Churches any more. We do not articulate their deepest hopes or highest ideals. Secularised man is no longer interested in understanding these in a Christian dimension.

It is in this context that Edward Norman especially castigates these leading writers and thinkers in the Churches who, instead of rejecting secularised ideas, have in fact adopted them and said that somehow, if you look at them in a particular way, these ideas are still Christian ones.[19] Here he comes close to Bryan Wilson's belief that the Churches cannot come to terms with contemporary society without completely abandoning their time-honoured values.

I have already stated my belief that Christians can come to grips with contemporary society and expect new insights for living today without abandoning our traditions or our faith in Jesus Christ. In doing so there is no need to capitulate to that society. There is a distinction between accepting secular humanism at its own valuation and what Owen Chadwick has described as 'the perpetual task of adjusting religious understanding of the world to new knowledge of the world.'[20] In today's society, however, the second task can be frightening. This is perhaps why over the last decade and more many in the Churches have busied themselves looking inward – reforming this bit of church government, rewriting this or that bit of our Sunday services, setting up committees, arguing whether or not we should unite with each other – doing endless jobs inside the house and never looking through the window to see what is happening in the world outside. It seems safer to remain irrelevant. Of course some of these matters have their importance. Indeed for many Christians worship, and especially the breaking of bread, the Holy Communion, is fundamental; but to concentrate so much attention on the way it is done, to go so far as to rewrite the Holy Communion service three times in one generation (as the Church of England has done) is surely to have become rather obsessed with externals and trivialities.

Archbishop Dwyer, the Roman Catholic Archbishop of Birmingham, makes the same point about his Church when he laments that anyone who reads the letter columns of the religious press will see 'how people tear themselves into tatters about Communion in the hand or God-knows-what, which couldn't have the slightest relevance to the vast majority of mankind.' According to Archbishop Dwyer Christians ought to be discussing the overriding threatening questions of the moment, such as unemployment and inflation, not ecclesiastical trivialities. If you are poor or unemployed, you are not likely to think that the Kingdom of God is about whether you receive Holy Communion in your hand or your mouth. You are much more likely to want to know whether Christianity has any good news for those who are suffering from inflation.

Another church leader, the Anglican Bishop of Liverpool David Sheppard, also makes relevance to the poor one way of testing whether the Churches are doing their work. Since in the Gospels a mark of the coming of the Messiah is that the poor have the good news proclaimed to them, David Sheppard holds that we can fairly test whether the Churches are reflecting authentically the life of Jesus by asking how they are helping (or not helping) those at the wrong end of society. He has, moreover, had the courage to spell this out in terms of housing, educational reform, worker participation and so on.[21]

Could it be, then, that what is being rejected today is not the Gospel but the irrelevance of the Churches precisely at those points where the Gospel should bite? Edward Norman has drawn attention to the extraordinary foolishness whereby 'Each generation of churchmen has appeared to imagine that it is the first to espouse social policies, the first to be concerned with the conditions of the working classes.'[22] Yet he himself admits[23] that the Church never caught up with the unprecedented problems caused by nineteenth-century capitalism, with its huge growth in population and its readiness to treat men and women as if they were machines. That failure in the past makes it more heinous today to shelter behind cosy irrelevancies instead of making it our total aim to look for the Kingdom of God and help others to find it.

In the light of all this are we right to be gloomy about the present health of the British Churches? I was surprised to find that David Martin is not particularly gloomy. Partly, he observes, his attitude is affected by the fact that the history of the Churches is filled with possibilities of doom; partly because the Churches' own theology leads us to expect them to be constantly on the edge of disaster. He compares the Church to those modern machines that are actually self-destructive. 'In a sense the Church has always been in the course of some kind of destruction in order to live again,' he says, 'some kind of death in order to achieve resurrection. Its whole relationship to society has been one of persistent deaths and resurrections. Its own theology tells it that it has to live through those over and over again.'

It remains true that nobody likes to die – though death is probably preferable to the possible future as depicted by Bryan Wilson. He does not believe that the Churches as institutions will disappear overnight. He thinks that there will continue to be religious people. The future of the Churches he sees as a sect. Some people would say that was its beginning; but Bryan Wilson is doubtful whether it will be as radical and challenging a sect as Christianity was in the beginning. What he pictures is sectarian groups inhabiting the ruins of the old church structure.

Bryan Wilson has himself observed that no completely secularized society yet exists.[26] It is difficult to envisage the consequences in such a society of the total elimination of the Churches and their clergy. No other bodies attempt to articulate man's whole place in the universe. No other group of persons exists to remind men and women of the life and work of Jesus Christ, and to break bread and share wine as he commanded. Nothing else aims to confront fallible human organisations with the claims of the eternal. Doctors, psychiatrists, social workers and others undoubtedly do sometimes serve as substitute figures for clergymen. No-one should mimimise the value of what they then can accomplish. (Indeed, one way in which clergymen have acknowledged this is by assimilating ideas and techniques of these professions.[25]) But important differences remain. Clergymen have different patterns of confidentiality from other counsellors as well as a far greater availability. Unlike the mental health agencies they are not simply concerned with what Bryan Wilson calls 'essentially private rehabiliation services for individuals with specific and acute problems'[26] but also with the general well-being of society. Their difficult calling is not primarily about social or medical engineering (however important these may be) but includes setting the whole of life in the context of faith – a faith which can also ecompass the failures as well as the successes of the psychiatrist, doctor, social worker or clergyman. And since that faith understood in the Christian tradition involves notions of solidarity and shared values, it cannot be explored alone, but only where there is a community whose members see themselves as called to seek the Kingdom of God and live as the salt of the earth.

Oddly enough it was the atheist Jill Tweedie who best expressed to me the loss to society of the disappearance of that community or its inability to do its proper work. I asked her if she knew of any organisation capable of replacing the Church. She replied. 'I can't think of any. I've joined and unjoined masses of organisations in my time, and I don't find any of them that can. You see, what the Church really stands for, should stand for, and which no one organisation can stand for, is the attempt to get at some truth. And it is a sort of overall truth that would help you to sort out the rest of your life, and your approaches to other people, and your political stance if you like. It is a centre which says: if you are a seeker after truth, then come.'

In some far less hospitable parts of the world the Church can still perform functions such as these. In Sofia a young university student explained to David Martin why she was in church: 'My father was a partisan but he doesn't object to my coming. I don't know whether God is real or not, but I come here to light a candle, to think, to be alone and to listen to the music. I cannot find the right word, but in the Church it is quiet and it is different.' David Martin comments that 'in a world of incessant inspirational songs and production targets and the endless ceremonial repetitions of the ideological jargon, there remains a region of personal being, sensitivity and experience of which the Church is now almost the sole institutional custodian.'[27]

That was in communist Bulgaria. In Britain are we so spiritually rich that we can afford to dispense with such an institution?

1. See for example William Rees-Mogg *An Humbler Heaven: the beginning of hope*, Hamish Hamilton 1977, and chapter 15, 'The Existence of God', in Peter Mullen *Beginning Philosophy*, Edward Arnold 1977.

2. Maurice B. Reckitt *Militant Here in Earth: Considerations on the prophetic function of the Church in the twentieth century*, Longmans 1957, p. 7.

3. Leslie Paul *The Deployment and Payment of the Clergy*, Church Information Office 1964, pp. 87 and 73.

4. David Martin *A Sociology of English Religion*, S.C.M. Press 1967, p. 120.

5. Malcolm Muggeridge *Tread Softly for You Tread on my Jokes*, Collins 1966, pp. 116f.

6. R. Currie, A. D. Gilbert and L. S. Horsley *Churches and Churchgoers: Patterns of Church growth in the British Isles since 1700*, Oxford University Press 1977 is invaluable here.

7. E. R. Norman *Church and Society in England 1770–1970: An historical study*, Oxford University Press 1976, p. 51.

8. See the tables, pp. 6–11, 16 and 234f., in B. R. Wilson *Religion in Secular Society*, C. A. Watts and Co., 1966.

9. *Social Trends No. 7*, Central Statistical Office 1976, p. 178, table 10.13; *Church of England Yearbook*, 1976, pp. 164f., table ix.

10. J. H. Newman *An Essay on the Development of Christian Doctrine* (1845), ed. J. M. Cameron, Pelican Books 1974, p. 176.

11. M. Martin *Three Popes and a Cardinal*, Hart- Davis 1973, p. 120.

12. The editor of *Theology*, discussing Leslie Paul *The Deployment and Payment of the Clergy*, *Theology* 67, No. 525, March 1964, p. 93.

13. On this see Owen Chadwick *The Secularization of the European Mind in the Nineteenth Century*, Cambridge University Press 1975, pp. 264ff.

14. 'Towards eliminating the concept of secularization', in *Penguin Survey of the Social Sciences 1965*, ed. J. Gould, Penguin Books 1965, pp. 182 and 169.

15. He adds, 'and a little more nonconformist and much less Anglican,' and then immediately adds some qualifications: *The Victorian Church: Part II*, A. & C. Black 1970, p. 221.

16. P. Althaus *Grundriss der Dogmatik*, Erlangen 1929, p. 19.

17. Eberhard Busch *Karl Barth, His Life from Letters and Autobiographical Texts*, tr. J. Bowden, S. C. M. Press 1976, p. 496.

18. The decline in attendance at political meetings, evening classes, youth clubs, theatres and cinemas was noticed in *Church and State. Report of the Archbishops' Commission*, Church Information Office 1970, p. 7.

19. He develops this indictment at length in chapter 10, 'After 1960', of
    Church and Society in England 1770–1970.
20. *The Secularization of the European Mind in the Nineteenth Century*, p. 15.
21. D. Sheppard *Built as a City: God and the urban world today*, Hodder and
    Stoughton 1974, pp. 160–7, 130–43 and 210–17.
22. *Church and Society in England 1770–1970*, p. 4.
23. *Ibid.*, p. 5.
24. *Religion in Secular Society*, p. 233.
25. See for example Roland Robertson *The Sociological Interpretation of Religion*,
    Basil Blackwell 1970, pp. 218ff.: 'Religion in relation to psychiatry and
    psychology'.
26. *Religion in Secular Society*, p. 73.
27. David Martin *The Religious and the Secular: Studies in Secularisation*,
    Routledge and Kegan Paul 1969, p. 152.

[2]
Facing the Facts

At the beginning of 1977 I asked Dr Stuart Mews, a sociologist at the University of Lancaster, to produce for me a set of statistics about the state of the British Churches. For any practising Christian his findings make gloomy reading.

On any average Sunday nearly 90 per cent of the population does not go to church. In England just over 90 per cent stay away, and in some urban areas in London and Birmingham the practice of Christian worship by the residential community has virtually ceased.

The main Free Churches in Britain are the Methodists, Baptists and the United Reformed Church, which together have lost 150 thousand members in the last seven years.

In four years the Church of Scotland has lost nearly 100 thousand members.

Over the last fifteen years the number of young people coming forward for confirmation in the Church of England has fallen by over a half. The Church of England ordained 600 new parsons in 1965; nine years later the same Church ordained only 400.

Between 1968 and 1973 the number of Roman Catholics attending Sunday Mass in this country fell by three hundred thousand.

Stuart Mews's figures seem to confirm that the total pattern for mainstream Christianity in Britain is decline. In that belief I decided to ask the leaders of the Churches what they are doing about it. Are they even facing the facts? And what is their reaction to them?

But facts can be disputed. Statistics are not everything. They might even be misleading. In the light of the figures produced by Stuart Mews I was surprised to discover that in 1976 the *Methodist Recorder* had proclaimed a 'steadying of nerve' in British Methodism and a boost of confidence in the local churches. Statistics supplied by the church membership secretary, the Revd Dr Bernard Jones, showed a 13 percent increase in the number of new members joining Methodism the previous year.[1]

What is the significance of such an increase? Is it just a flash in the pan, or is it likely to continue? Has Methodism got something the other Churches lack? I decided to ask Dr Bernard Jones first of all to be more precise about the figures. He told me that the increase in new members in 1975 (amounting to almost 11,000 converts) was the first such increase since 1962, and that he expected such increases to be repeated.

Because the figures presented by the Methodists seem so unusual in the light of what is happening in the other Churches I also asked Stuart Mews about them. Although he himself is a member of the Methodist Church, Dr Mews felt far less optimistic than Dr Jones. For one thing, he points out, the 13 per cent increase in 1975 over the previous year conceals the fact that in the same year 12,500 people ceased to be members, and the total loss in the denomination as a whole was 15,731 – the largest loss in membership since 1971. Moreover, in 1975 the Methodist Church made 1,000 fewer new members than it did in 1972. 'The figures taken as a whole,' says Stuart Mews, 'are not as encouraging as perhaps Dr Jones has indicated.'

So matters aren't so bright among the British Methodists after all. In fact, Bernard Jones himself admits that the bulk of the new membership is being gathered in only a fifth of the Methodist churches. What is happening, I wonder, in those churches that are not producing new members?

Whatever the case, it is clear that Methodism is not immune from the problems facing the other British Churches. Dr Bernard Jones is well aware that many people received into membership soon lapse. One of the main reasons, he thinks, is the social mobility that breaks up people's roots in a church community. 'They move from the neighbourhood and begin to go to a new Church, but don't last.' But why in 1976 did the Methodist church leadership play down these depressing facts? As Stuart Mews says, '*The Methodist Recorder* and the Connexional leadership[2] have tended to place a great deal of emphasis on one particular set of figures which seem very encouraging, whereas a total picture is far from encouraging.' He believes that the Connexional leadership at the present time is attempting to promote an 'ideology of success' to boost morale, and that this could be extremely dangerous. Such an ideology hides the reality of the situation. Stuart Mews believes that the picture is gloomy enough to make it 'unlikely that Methodism is going to survive into the next century.'

Here Bernard Jones disagrees. Statistically the prospects may look like that; but he thinks there will still be a Church, 'if not Methodism, something like Methodism.' It may not be numerically strong, but its influence will be strong. 'It could well be', he says, 'that we shall reach some level where we have a smaller Church, but a Church of convinced people,'

That I believe to be realistic. Church people do not have to hide from reality. We can face the facts of numerical decline and still look forward to a Church which might have a lot of impact. But it troubles me very much to find some Church leadership giving the impression that all is well, dangerously boosting our confidence in the way described by Stuart Mews. And it is not only some Methodists who are hiding from the facts. The Anglican Bishop of Liverpool, David Sheppard, told me he believes that quite a lot of people in his own Church are unwilling to face the reality of the situation.

In the 1960s David Sheppard worked with considerable success as warden and chaplain of the Mayflower Family Centre in Canning Town. (He also, with less success, captained the English cricket eleven in the 1963 Test series against Australia.)[3] Now Bishop of Liverpool, he recognises that an enormous number of people, in the big cities in particular, have grown up entirely outside the life of the Churches.[4] 'We completely misunderstand the situation,' he told me, in his tiny office in the heart of Liverpool, with the traffic rolling by outside, 'if we think that we're in a position where we can call people back to some faith or understanding that they once had.'

It is refreshing to come across a man in the Churches' leadership who is not displaying an unreasonable optimism, who perceives that the British Churches are now in what an older gereration would have called a missionary situation. What astonished me was to find Church leaders who regard the decline in Church allegiance as, in some respects, a good thing.

One such leader is Dr Mervyn Stockwood, Anglican Bishop of Southwark since 1959. His diocese stretches along the Thames from Kingston to Woolwich and reaches south into Surrey as far as Gatwick airport. In the 1960s the Revd Nick Stacey made a survey of confirmations in the diocese and concluded that if the rate of decline continued there would be no confirmations at all in Southwark by the mid-1970s.[5] In fact 2,511 persons were confirmed there in 1974 (though this was over 300 fewer than in 1971 and relates to a diocese containing between two and three million people).[6] Nick Stacey was wrong – but not far wrong.

Mervyn Stockwood himself has no illusions about the situation of the Churches in his part of Britain; but when I asked him why he thinks fewer people are attaching themselves to organised religion, the reasons he gave were greatly to people's credit. First, he believes that superstition has declined. 'When I started my ministry,' he told me, '95 per cent of the parish was baptized. People never came to church. They just had to have their kid "done".' Now he thinks people are better educated. Secondly, the Church is very much stricter now, especially with regard to confirmation. 'I used to be very uneasy when I was first bishop,' he recalled, 'with all these kids coming up for confirmation. As somebody once said, "They've come on another night of perjury, making all those promises without knowing what they mean".' Now, says Mervyn Stockwood, confirmands are much more committed. Obviously in his view the old days were in some respects bad old days. Better education, the decline of superstition about religion, a stricter Church, these changes certainly could be producing fewer Christians – but more committed ones.

And at the other end of Britain, in Edinburgh University, I found that the Revd Dr Andrew Ross, a Church of Scotland Minister, also has no desire to go back to the days when churches were filled. At that time, in his view, the Churches were in danger of being mere chaplains to the Establishment: instead of seeking the Kingdom of God the Church too often blessed what it should have condemned. Andrew Ross would regard a return to the old church-going days as a 'wholly bad thing'. To go back to a 'complacent well-attended church, unaware of the terrible problems around it would be a worse crisis than half-empty churches today.' The corollary of this for Dr Ross is that the Churches should be a force for the good life here on earth, quite apart from what happens after death. 'The crisis for me', he says, 'is that so many church-goers in Scotland do not see the role the Church should be playing in Scottish society.' Well-attended churches may be complacent churches.

Everthing clearly depends on how the statistics are interpreted. Looking at the facts honestly we cannot avoid the truth that numbers are declining in most Churches in Britain. But as the Revd Dr Colin Morris puts it: 'Some would say that these statistics prove that the Church is on the way out. Others would say that the Church is losing an awful lot of accumulated fat and might be a much leaner, maybe even hungrier, but healthier institution as a consequence.'

I met Colin Morris when he was President of the Methodist Conference, in his office at the headquarters of the Methodist Missionary Society. On one wall was a picture of a charging rhinoceros, to remind him of the 17 years he spent in Zambia; on a bookcase was a polished pit lamp to remind him that his father was a Lancashire miner. I put it to him that if the Churches are losing some of their accumulated fat, we ought by now to be seeing some signs of renewed life. He diagnoses however, another weakness of today's Churches: ecclesiastical hypochondria. Each Church is continually taking its own pulse and its own temperature and using the data which result from this operation not merely to determine the presence or absence of the Kingdom of Heaven (i.e. if the membership increases the Kingdom of Heaven is at hand; if the membership declines, it's tarrying), but also to determine the state of God's health. 'I think', said Colin Morris, 'that there are very devout Methodists who are quite convinced that in the dying breath of the last Methodist God will in some way disappear in a puff of pink smoke for ever.'

What makes this preoccupation so dangerous in Colin Morris's view is that it distorts the true relationship between the Churches and the Kingdom of God. The Churches are the servants of the Kingdom. 'It's the Kingdom we've got to keep our eye on,' he says, 'and the presence of the Kingdom in everyday life And this constant analysis of and moaning about the state of the Church is not likely to lead us to ask the questions that are really important.'

Christians believe that the Kingdom of God calls us to try to create a just and humane society, that God is actually working in the world to bring this about, and that we can co-operate with him The Kingdom of God is to be found where men and women in their working lives, in their family lives, in their politics and in their personal relationships are actually seeking God's will. As far as the Churches are concerned, facing the facts involves looking at ourselves as we are, reduced in numbers, leaner, hungrier, perhaps more convinced, more committed – and then asking how we as Churches can serve the Kingdom of God.

Colin Morris speaks of how a Christian must be passionate about all the issues of life in our society. We must not be selectively compassionate, limiting our concern simply to what takes our fancy.[7] At the same time, I felt, he combines his seriousness about the Kingdom of God with a measure of light-heartedness about the future of the Churches. People are beginning to see, he maintains, that the survival of the Churches is not the basic issue. In his view the New Testament is not desperately concerned about the survival of the Church, or at all with the question of how *we* are doing. The New Testament, says Colin Morris, 'is concerned with the question about God at work in the world: what is *He* doing and where is He doing it and where can we take our stand alongside Him.'

If you distinguish as clearly as Colin Morris does between the Kingdom of God and the Churches, it is probably not difficult to contemplate their disappearance; but no other Church leader I met is as willing to go so far as Dr Morris in this respect. In fact, Archbishop Dwyer (who as chairman of the Catholic Bishops leads the Roman Catholic Church in Britain) came close to identifying the Church with 'the Kingdom of God which Christ has already founded, started in the world now to be perfected in eternity.' The Kingdom of God is the Church, he said; 'but all men who are in a state of grace are associated with that in some way, and we don't limit, can't limit the grace of God simply to church members.' If you do see God's Kingdom so closely identified with a Church, it is much harder to contemplate the death of that Church.

Yet Archbishop Dwyer is well aware of decline. Our age he describes as one of 'recession' in the Church. Even now his own diocese is short of priests and soon the manpower shortage will be serious.

Facing these facts has made the Archbishop interestingly optimistic. In his view this shortage of priests is going to let other members of the Church come into their own at last. For example, the worshippers now kneeling in the pews are going to start running the Church's services themselves.

I asked him how this would apply to the Mass, which for Catholics is the central act of worship that can bind a church community together. Catholics hold that only a priest can celebrate the Eucharist and offer the Sacrifice of the Mass. But the sacrament can be reserved, to be distributed in Holy Communion to the faithful later. Archbishop Dwyer envisages that if there is no priest available the people will gather for what is called the liturgy of the Word, the first part of the Mass which includes Bible reading, prayer, a homily and so on. 'For the second part it would be a lay person who would give Holy Communion, and they would have a Communion Service – not Mass but a Communion Service. And that could be done entirely by the laity if there weren't a priest about,' says the Archbishop.

Now if we are going to see laymen (and women, perhaps) giving Holy Communion in Roman Catholic churches in Britain, I do not think the movement will end there. Those who are taking such responsibility in the churches because there is no priest available are bound to want, even demand, other responsibilities as well. According to Archbishop Dwyer this is already happening in some parts of the Catholic world. He quoted a parish priest in France who has told his congregation, 'I'm the last parish priest that's coming here. When I die there is nobody else to send in my place. There will be a priest to circulate from time to time; but for the most part you'll just have to run the parish yourselves.'

Interestingly, Colin Morris also turned to another part of the world when he wanted to indicate how Churches in this country might forge ahead. Having spent 17 years as a missionary in Africa he tossed aside most of my statistics about the decline of the Churches in Britain. He believes that facing all the facts means looking at the rest of the world as well and trying to learn from it. In a world-wide sense, he claims, the Church is booming. Here in Britain we should stop thinking negatively of shrinkage and ask ourselves how to make a greater impact. That would change our patterns of worship; it would change our style of ministry; it would change our whole perspective of our role in society. He points out that although some of the African Churches are booming, they still cannot afford vast numbers of clergy. As a result the laity there have had to learn how to stand on their own feet.

These, then, are the responses to the facts of declining church membership that I found among representative Church leaders. Some are absurdly optimistic. Others look for a leaner, yet healthier Church that is really seeking the Kingdom of God rather than worrying about its own well-being. Others look towards a new breed of lay Christian who will take over responsibilities that the fast-disappearing clergymen once jealously guarded as their own preserves.

But where will such laity come from in Britain, when most Christian congregations are also slowly disappearing? Dr John Robinson, who used to be Bishop of Woolwich and is now Dean of Trinity College, Cambridge, feels that this is the very point where the Churches must mobilise their resources, that man-power which at present remains idle in the pews. He thinks most of this has got to be done at the small-scale level, training and equipping more or less the whole body of committed Christians to see that they are really in the ministry, and that a great part of their ministry is going to be done where they work. He naintains that at the moment we have 'a sort of one-type soldier army', with most Christians not thinking of themselves as in the ministry at all. To develop a better understanding of ministry among the whole Christian body demands considerable imagination and good theology in the Churches' leadership.

In the opinion of Mervyn Stockwood the Church in general is not ready for such a recovery of spirit. He spells out his own version of Colin Morris's 'ecclesiastical hypochondria'. He told me that what worries him is the 'endless committees and masses of paper' giving an analysis of why people don't go to church. 'If some of my own clergy who go around to their endless committees and yak and yak and yak away would only get on with the job of trying to convert their own parishioners, I think that we should not be in quite the state of decline that we are.' Mervyn Stockwood describes committees, paper-work and bureaucracy as 'three of the devil's favourite weapons for stopping the Christian doing his work as an evangelist.' Facing the facts for Dr Stockwood means cutting ourselves free from a lot of that. Otherwise the future is bleak.

Bishop David Sheppard is, I think, even more pessimistic; because of course if the Churches manage to get rid of those endless committees and start concentrating on Jesus Christ instead, we still have to face what is often a hostile world. In David Sheppard I found a mixture of realism, pessimism and trust in God. Facing the gloomy facts includes for him looking among them for flickers of light. In spite of his pessimism (and realism) about the prospects of the Churches in urban areas, he thanks God that he sees evidence in his diocese that God is alive at work. And he believes that 'when Christians reflect his life of caring and presence in the middle of life, then people will take Jesus Christ very seriously indeed.'

It is important here to ask whether a reading of the Gospels makes us expect any kind of success, or whether Jesus envisaged his followers as anything more than a minority. But however we answer those questions, they do not excuse the inadequacies of our present Church life. It is a flicker of light that some of our Church leaders are closely aware of the problems. Without a wide enough vision of what the Churches should be, we shall just plod on into the ground. New patterns of ministry will not arise of their own accord. They need fostering, as do the new patterns of clergy to go with them. In a later chapter I examine whether we are training our clergy for yesterday's or tomorrow's churches. More of our Church leaders need to open their eyes (and our eyes) to the facts not only about the British Churches but also the wider Church outside this island, so that (as Archbishop Dwyer has learned from France and Colin Morris from Africa) we can start to learn ways of coping with situations that so far have stumped the Churches in Britain.

I was surprised to find Mervyn Stockwood implying that our British problems are more intractable than those of the younger Churches. He was telling me of his hopes for a spiritual revival and the frustrations arising from our history, our buildings and legalities which, he said, we cannot just get rid of like that. It would be different, said Dr Stockwood, 'if we were to find ourselves in a new country – shall we say in Africa? – where you travel lightly.'

In my view travelling lightly is the right phrase to describe how Churches reduced in numbers and wealth might operate effectively in this country. I look forward to it. Facing the facts means accepting the notion of smaller Churches containing more committed Christians. This is turn means shedding a lot of paraphernalia, like too much bureaucracy and too many buildings. And it means the disappearance of that army of parsons who made people forget that being a full-time Christian is every church member's job; and that the Kingdom of God is to be sought where people live and work and suffer as well as in church.

Yet I still ask whether there are any points of growth now in the British churches. Sometimes people have mentioned to me, as I have been researching this book, the movement called Pentecostalism. Other people have called it the charismatic movement. According to the Bible a charisma is a special gift of grace bestowed on a Christian for his work; and the charismatic movement, I was told, consists of Christians who are filled with such gifts and are themselves filling churches of many different sorts and traditions.

For a good number of Church leaders what is happening here is more than a 'flicker of light'. In Colin Morris's opinion these churches are full, not because they have superlative orators in the pulpit, but because people come with a sense of expectancy that something is going to happen in that hour which could change the whole course of their lives. If there are such places in Britain today, if that is a fact of British church life, we need to look at them.

1. *The Methodist Recorder*, 8 July 1976, pp.1 and 7.
2. i.e. the secretary of the Methodist Conference, the heads of the various Divisions of the Conference and similar officials. This group does not include the President of the Conference, who customarily retires from the office after a year's service.
3. D. Sheppard *Parson's Pitch*, Hodder and Stoughton 1964. For the disappointing Test series, p.235.
4. David Sheppard's *Built as a City*, Hodder and Stoughton 1974, published after he had become bishop but mostly written out of his Canning Town experiences, contains many insights into the problems of Christianity in large conurbations.
5. N. Stacey *Who Cares?*, Anthony Blond 1971, pp.302f.
6. *Church of England Year Book 1976*, 1976, pp.164f.
7. For some of Colin Morris's concerns see for example his book *Unyoung, Uncoloured, Unpoor*, Epworth Press 1969.

[3]
The Disturbing Spirit

Colin Morris misled me when he suggested that worship in Pentecostal or 'charismatic' churches lasts only an hour. Sometimes this is the case. At other times the intensity of feeling is so great that worship goes on and on. But nobody yawns or looks at his watch. The sense of expectation does not allow it.

For more staid Christians it can also be alarming when someone in such a service begins to speak out in a language he or she does not understand, a language moreover that those listening probably do not understand. This is in fact a twentieth-century equivalent of something that used to happen in New Testament times. The first time it happened was on the day of Pentecost, or Whit Sunday, when (according to the Acts of the Apostles) the disciples of Jesus were all filled with the Holy Spirit and began to speak in other tongues.[1] Even then people thought they were mad or drunk. And the phenomenon remains disturbing today, especially to the reserved British in their churches. Others welcome it as a charismatic gift of great value.

In this century the first people who began to talk like this in churches were American negroes. They called themselves Pentecostalists. In their church meetings they believed that the Holy Spirit empowered them to perform healings as well. Most of the more traditional Churches rejected them at the time; so they remained independent, though they did spread to other countries. In this country the best-known Pentecostal Churches are the Assemblies of God and the Elim Four Square Gospel Church. In addition there are very many Pentecostal, or Pentecostal-like, Churches filled entirely by black immigrants or their families. According to Dr Stuart Mews, one-fifth of the black population of Britain belongs to a black Church,[2] with little or no contact with other worshipping communities.

For a long time these Churches remained small. Pentecostalism attracted only a tiny minority of Christians in Britain. Then in the 1950s it began to spill over into the older Churches. Presbyterians, Anglicans, Roman Catholics and others too began to find a new spontaneity in their worship. 'Speaking with tongues' (or glossolalia), previously unheard of in many a staid church, now began to embarrass some congregations – and some of their clergy. Others became enthusiastic, especially at first in the United States. By the end of the 1960s over 10,000 American Roman Catholics, for instance, had experienced this speaking with tongues.[3] They called it baptism in the Spirit.

The movement affected clergy and laity, the unlettered and the highly educated. An American Jesuit, Donald Gelpi, records how over breakfast at Fordham University in 1968 he learned about this new Catholic Pentecostalism from a fellow Jesuit.

> While he talked, I felt deeply moved. After breakfast, I felt almost physically drawn to the chapel, where I sat down to pray. Following Jim's description of his own gift of tongues, I began to say quietly to myself: 'La, la, la, la.' To my immense consternation, there ensued a rapid movement of tongue and lips, accompanied by a tremendous feeling of inner devotion. I can look back on that experience as a turning-point in my own spiritual development.[4]

Now the movement is affecting the British Churches too. Bishop Mervyn Stockwood told me there are something like 70 clergy in his diocese who are either interested in it or claim to have had some sort of experience of healing or speaking in tongues. 'I cannot speak too highly of their contribution,' he says. 'I've seen parishes brought to life as result of it.'

That congregations are initially startled at some manifestations of the charismatic movement is understandable. The Revd John Farmborough described to me how, one Whit Sunday, he had introduced speaking in tongues to his congregation. First he talked about the whole subject of the gifts of the

Holy Spirit. Then he spoke in Portuguese, a language he understands though most of his congregation do not. Thirdly he spoke in tongues, not understanding himself the meaning of what he was saying. But, he explains, 'I was saying something to God which I thought He wanted me to say, because it was to His glory in some way.'

In part embarrassment at this kind of behaviour arises simply because glossolalia is an unfamiliar religious symbol. 'Glossolalia says: God is here, just as a Gothic cathedral says: God is majestic, or the eucharistic bread says: Jesus is *realiter* here,' explains Professor Walter Hollenweger. He adds that 'Glossolalia builds up a social acoustic sanctuary, a cathedral of sounds, for people who do not have a Gothic cathedral (and that is the majority of the Christians in the Third World), or who have left it (and that is the great part of the Christians in the Western World).'[5]

John Farmborough believes speaking in tongues is also a sign that the Holy Spirit is bestowing gifts on Christians, and that for many years men and women in the Churches have been seeking to serve God without these necessary gifts. He holds that the charismatic movement is in accord with what God offers in the Bible to His people. 'It is certainly the way forward for me,' he says.

And it is not simply *inside* churches that some Christians are beginning to worship God in this way. Although some people claim to posses the ability to explain or interpret what a person means when speaking in tongues, in church there remains a problem of understanding. For this reason a number of people who do worship God in this way do not do so publicly. A doctor's wife in Nottingham told me that for her the private exercise of the gift of tongues is the most important part of her personal relationship with the Lord, though she will not express herself in this way in public. She sees the need for a combination of this way of worship and other liturgical patterns. 'We don't throw out the liturgy just because we've got something new coming in,' she comments, 'but we can marry both the old and the new.'

Clearly in one way or another something striking and exciting is happening to a lot of people in the British Churches because of this movement. The older Pentecostal Churches still exist; but these special gifts of the Spirit which used to be confined to them – speaking in (or 'with') tongues especially, but also, some claim, healing the sick as well are being exercised by Christians in other denominations now. Through this some Christians and churches are obviously coming alive again. Small wonder if some churchmen look to the movement as the way towards revival.

Speaking in tongues which few understand ought also to have a particularly strong appeal to many people in a class-ridden society such as ours. This may help to account for the fact that Pentecostalism can bring together very diverse people. Professor David Martin pointed out to me that language usually *separates* people in Britain: they are branded by accent. 'Obviously if you have a belief in tongues that transcend ordinary language,' he observes, 'that crosses the social barriers to some extent as well.'

I picked up an entertaining confirmation of the point that Pentecostalists may well be extremely conscious of class barriers outside their churches in the selection of letters to Archbishop Donald Coggan published after the Archbishops' Call to the Nation in 1976. A correspondent belonging to what he described as 'a classless Pentecostal church' in the Home Counties wrote, 'The reason the Church of England churches are being emptied is because of people like you who associate with the earls, lords, kings and ruling classes and then call upon ordinary people to make sacrifices.'[6]

David Martin also suggests that one cause of the movement's rapid development in the 1960s lies in its relationship to a general feature of British society at that time. In the 1960s every kind of structure, and especially role structures (such as minister and congregation, or bureaucrat and ordinary person) came to be seen as restrictive. It was felt, as David Martin says, 'that to get rid of the ordinary restrictions of language and the ordinary restrictions of roles would make you really encounter people directly and for that matter encounter God directly.' Pentecostalism, with its relative freedom from such restrictions, benefitted from this notion of the structures of society constricting and oppressing us.

Of course there is nothing specifically religious about that; but it seems to me to be one of the few points where what has been happening in our society in general actually works in favour of a religious revival and not against one.[7] Reflecting that particular trend in society, Pentecostalism was (and perhaps still is) more likely to win adherents than most other religious movements.

Pentecostalism also possesses, I think, a religious element that is bound to appeal to a number of people today simply because we live in such an uncertain world. Many now find it difficult to know whether or not they can still believe in the old-time religion. The Pentecostal movement offers a kind of security precisely because it makes no compromises on this. It takes Christianity straight, so to speak, without any watering down. In taking literally the gifts of the Spirit described in the New Testament it takes the Bible itself very literally indeed.

Dr Bryan Wilson sees this as a double-edged asset, for most people (both inside and outside the Churches) do not now find acceptable a position that sets out so uncompromisingly the old-time values based on the old-time stories. He thinks Pentecostalists take the Scriptures far too literally for most Christians, though he concedes that a section of the population finds this authority, this literalness, extremely attractive.

For such reasons it could be that the movement might not simply revive some congregations; it might also divide them. The Revd John Farmborough frankly admits that this has happened in his own church. There have been what he calls 'some remarkable conversions' and more people are coming to the church. But some are staying away because, says John Farmborough, 'it's not like what they were used to.' He refuses to judge them. If they do not feel happy about it at the moment, he believes they will eventually change their minds.

There is, nonetheless, a danger that some Christians are

going to feel themselves to be second-class citizens if they do not have some of these particular gifts. And if you do not have the gift of tongues or of interpreting them, you could well feel irritated by those who claim to have been set on fire in this way. At St John's Theological College, Nottingham, I heard a sharp exchange on the subject between two men training for the Church of England ministry. One was explaining that through the charismatic movement he has entered into a completely new, radically powerful experience of God. His colleague countered that he felt uncomfortable and unhelped by such spiritual gifts. 'I don't crave them,' he said. 'I don't feel anything is said of any value generally or personally to me in what is called tongues or the interpretation of them.' The first ordinand retorted: 'Maybe that says more about you than about the gifts.'

No members of the charismatic movement would actually say that if you do not possess these gifts you are a second-class Christian. But the logic of what they say leads to that conclusion: if you do not find such gifts helpful, that says something about your own spiritual inadequacy. In fact I think this kind of division happened in the early Church too. St Paul was obliged to deal with it. Mervyn Stockwood thinks that bishops ought to be alert to use St Paul's remedy in these religious rows. St Paul wrote of 'a more excellent way', the way of love. Love, says Mervyn Stockwood, 'is one mark of the spirit which is obligatory. The other gifts of the Spirit, whether healings or speaking in tongues or prophecy, are God's gifts and some have them and some haven't; but the love is something which every Christian must experience and radiate.'

If, however, Mervyn Stockwood interprets St Paul rightly, the gifts which this charismatic movement is stressing are not the most important ones for a Christian, and it is unbalanced to emphasise them too much. More, the bishop clearly feels the need to keep an eye on this charismatic movement in his Church, as if it might get out of hand. Bryan Wilson believes that the church authorities in general are a little embarrassed by the movement. On the one hand they see that it is one of the few exciting things to have happened within the Churches in the last 20 years; on the other hand they are not sure what it all purports in the long run. Dr Wilson thinks their embarrassment is understandable, because the implications of charismatic renewal taken to the full would break down the structures of the Churches. 'If the ordinary individual can receive power of a spiritual kind from God in an unmediated way,' he explains, 'then one must begin to question the role of the priest. One must begin to say, "Why do we need priests when the Holy Ghost moves directly in us and through us?"'

Church leaders are not altogether ready to take seriously the theological implications of a movement which might lead to this kind of change. The fact that they (or anyone) may be embarrassed by something does not make it wrong. It takes time to adjust to new ideas, especially when they seem to be causing a ferment. In the end the church leaders may well come down on the side of the Pentecostal movement in their Churches, in spite of an initial caution. I found the Roman Catholic Archbishop of Liverpool, Derek Worlock, doing precisely that: being cautious but in the end coming out in favour of what is happening. He refuses to take absolutely at face value everything that is calling itself Pentecostalism. Certain aspects of enthusiasm in its wilder states do not necessarily benefit a community; similarly, the presence of the Spirit in the Church need not mean that to express it in a completely free way is to the advantage of the Church. 'There's got to be a certain co-ordination and development,' he says, 'and therefore, as St Paul suggests, even those who have this gift of the Spirit at times may need to restrain it a little, so as to be able to bring all the other members with it.'

Yet Derek Worlock adds that generally what is happening in the Churches because of the movement is good and hopeful. 'There's always got to be caution,' he maintains; 'but if it's a choice between caution and opening yourself to the Spirit, then I'll open myself to the Spirit any day.'

Even so, that begs the question whether or not this is a genuine movement of the Spirit in the British Churches. One Roman Catholic who has made a special study of Pentecostalism is Fr Simon Tugwell, a Dominican priest from Oxford. He has doubts as well as praise. He is most impressed by the diversity of expression within Pentecostal worship. Some ministers dress in Roman collars that would not be out-of-place in the Roman curia, delivering themselves of basic home truths in the most straightforward way; others sing and shout their homily with gusto and apparent abandon. In a typical congregation some kneel and say their prayers quietly, while others dance round, laughing and singing, neither getting in each other's way. 'People are expressing themselves in a way that is natural to them, but they're not rounding anybody up,' says Simon Tugwell. 'There are Pentecostal churches where there's a tremendous sense of what you might call a disciplined freedom.'

Disciplined freedom, in which people can have their say and worship how and when they want to, is not found in many other Churches. For one thing most traditional Churches are hamstrung by legalities that would rule out any really experimental approach to the worship of God, however disciplined by the worshippers themselves.

Simon Tugwell's praise, however, applies to the Pentecostal Churches, which he believes to be far healthier than the movement that has spilled over into other denominations. In the Pentecostal Churches he holds that there is a much greater insight into what a whole Christian ought to be, whereas elsewhere the movement has led people to 'specialise' in only part of the Christian gospel. Some people, he thinks, respond to Pentecostalism as a way of avoiding the whole dimension of suffering, of crucifixion, that is part of Christianity. They hold on to what may be a very profound experience of joy, of being freed from a certain kind of burden, and they will not let go of it.

Simon Tugwell admits that in Roman Catholicism until fairly recently the cross was probably stressed almost too much: 'if you weren't suffering then you weren't really a good Christian; the more you hated your religious life, the better a religious you were.' He now thinks there is a danger of the pendulum swinging to the other extreme, for an essential part of living in this world (and therefore of living in the Church in the world) is that our experience varies. We are happy one day and miserable the next, and all of that is within the Lord's providence and within the Lord's blessing. Not only does Simon Tugwell believe that the charismatic movement tends to forget this; he also maintains that it can set up a real kind of Phariseeism, 'always telling people that they must be happy the whole time, that if they're not happy they're losing the faith and losing the Spirit.'

He also thinks that some charismatics do not always mean what they say. They have learned a jargon that comes ultimately from the Pentecostal churches. They speak of baptism in the Holy Spirit, and then 'flowing from that' a semi-technical use of a whole range of words connected with joy and freedom from anxiety. Simon Tugwell is unconvinced by the confident way some charismatics use these words. 'They say how they've been freed from all their anxieties, when they're manifestly sitting there very tense and worried about everything,' he says. They are clutching at the language, he believes, precisely because they are *not* relaxed and freed from their cares.

As a result he sees a psychological pitfall in the movement, since it avoids the whole dimension of suffering in life. It offers a kind of short-cut through life which does not in the end lead anywhere.

That harsh judgement could explain why some people have tended to drift away from the movement after a while. As I was looking for Churches where this charismatic movement has made a difference, I came across some that are going through what one Pentecostal vicar described to me as 'a kind of trough'. Obviously a movement lacking in that side of the Christian faith which enables us to cope with continuing ill-health or unhappiness cannot satisfy people for ever.

Dr Bryan Wilson has found some evidence that this is a movement to which people come and then gradually drift out of, without ever disbelieving. He suggests that the experience of charismatic renewal may become too repetitive, too uncumulative, leading to 'nothing except periodic gratifications of a spiritual kind which in the modern world are difficult to sustain.'

That may be so if we consider the movement in isolation. I do not think the charismatic movement possesses enough resources to sustain people for a lifetime in the service of God. It has much to offer the traditional Churches, yet by itself it is not enough. There is far more to the Christian gospel than speaking in tongues, healing the sick by laying on hands with prayer, and feeling a sense of peace and happiness. And I think also that the Pentecostal attitude to the Bible – the movement's fundamentalism, as the theologians term it – will not suffice for thinking men and women today. Professor Walter Hollenweger, a Christian who greatly admires the Pentecostal Churches, dedicates his book about them:

> To my friends and teachers in the Pentecostal Movement
> who taught me to love the Bible
> And to my teachers and friends in the Presbyterian Church
> who taught me to understand it.[8]

Happily there is evidence that British Pentecostalists (no doubt partly through contact with other Churches) are coming to grips with Biblical scholarship.[9]

For these reasons it seems to me that this disturbing movement of the Pentecostal Spirit in the Churches will not in the end by itself bring about revival in the Churches. Yet I do not wish to leave it at that negative point. Many of the people I met in the movement are sincere and loving people – some of them obviously set on fire to work for God's Kingdom. Can the Churches as a whole learn nothing from them?

Oddly enough Simon Tugwell, who was more critical of them than anyone else I talked with, turns their rather narrow view of the Bible into a kind of gain. They have, he says, a freedom in using the Bible which is fascinating. They do not feel bound by the literal sense, but neither do they feel bound by what the scholars say, by academic respectability. As Simon Tugwell puts it, they believe 'this is the living word of God and it says whatever it wants to say.' Professor David Martin, too, countered my criticism of the Pentecostalists' fundamentalism by observing that in returning to the Bible, they gain more than they lose by taking it so literally. 'There are huge archaic ancient symbols lying there to which the Pentecostalist refers back,' argues Professor Martin. 'The fact that he does it in a fundamentalist frame is of no particular consequence.'

Certainly the use of the Bible in this way not only gives a sense of security. It also gives the believer a flexible, new and inspiring language, filled with images and the fundamental symbols of religion, like fire and wind and tongues. Here the Pentecostal Churches can remind us of the roots of our religion. And they can bring an equally valuable gift to our worship by reminding us that God can speak to us through our own physical selves. That can help to make us more whole as human beings.

Pentecostalists use the body a great deal in worship. Because of this Simon Tugwell believes that his own Catholic Church can be renewed by contact with the Pentecostal Churches. They have, he says, 'rediscovered processions for instance, rediscovered candles; they've rediscovered gesture, they've rediscovered ritual, I think (though they probably wouldn't like the word).' This is, he believes, a rediscovery of the sacramental principle, and he adds that 'this is surely a very important part of our rediscovering our own roots as Catholics.'

That is a handsome tribute. Pentecostalism is a growing force in the Churches outside Britain, but for too long the Pentecostal Churches have been outsiders in this country. In latching on to the great imagery of Christianity, imagery of fire and wind and tongues; in teaching us to express our worship physically; in drawing us to take the Bible seriously again; in loosening up our church structures and teaching us that anyone can be filled with the Spirit and has a right to speak and be heard; in all these ways Pentecostalism can give us some new life. It is not the answer to all our problems; but it is a breath of fresh air in stale churches.

1. Acts 2. 4.
2. See Roswith Gerloff 'Black Christian communities in Birmingham', in Alan Bryman (ed.) *Religion in Birmingham*, Birmingham University

Institute for the Study of Worship and Religious Architecture, 1975.
3. Walter J. Hollenweger *The Pentecostals,* S.C.M. Press 1969, p.15.
4.   Quoted by Don Cupitt 'The Charismatic Illusion' in *The Listener,* 22 July 1976, p.77. This short piece is extremely hostile to the charismatic movement.
5. W. Hollenweger 'Creator Spiritus: the challenge of Pentecostal experience to Pentecostal theology,' in *Theology,* 71 No.679, January 1978, p.37.
6. John Poulton *Dear Archbishop,* Hodder and Stoughton 1976, p.132.
7. Cf. 'Spontaneity and subjectivism have become powerful elements in contemporary culture. Inner feeling has been widely hailed as more *authentic* than intellectual knowledge . . . It should not surprise us if, against the general background of secularization, the one 'growth sector' within the Churches and within institutionalized religion should mobilize the same dispositions.' Bryan Wilson *Contemporary Transformations of Religion,* Oxford University Press 1976, p.37.
8. *The Pentecostals,* p.xvi.
9. See for example the essays in *Pentecostal Doctrine,* ed. P. S. Brewster, Grenehurst Press, Cheltenham 1976.

[4]
The Outsiders

Colin Barnett is a full-time Trade Union officer, a short stocky man of tremendous physical and intellectual energy. He consciously tries to link his work with the Christian faith. But in terms of the Churches he describes himself as 'undoubtedly an outsider – who might well wish to be an insider, but would only be an insider if the Church changed its attitudes.' He sits, as he puts it, 'very much on the periphery of the Church.'

That, I believe, describes a great many people in Britain today, especially manual workers and industrial workers, sitting very much on the periphery of the Churches, outsiders. 'Outsider' is not a particularly nice word; but I want to use it not only of those who have never really belonged to a Church but also of those who once belonged and have walked out.

Such a person is Charles Davis who, amid much publicity, resigned the Roman Catholic priesthood in 1967. He feels still that the administrative organisation of the Church has a wrong structure and understanding of itself that has in fact destructive effects on people. This out-of-date hierarchical structure is preventing the life of the Church from truly developing.

Charles Davis became professor of religion at Concordia University, Montreal. He is now married and has children of his own. Although he remains a Christian, in terms of the official hierarchy of the Roman Catholic Church he is an outsider. But for his part he believes that the Church as it exists and works at present is an obstacle in the lives of the committed Christian he most admires. 'It is not the source of the values they cherish and promote. On the contrary, they live and work in constant tension and opposition to it.' In a phrase strikingly reminiscent of Colin Barnett's, he asserts that many manage to remain members only because they are able to live their Christian lives 'on the fringe of the institutional Church.'[1]

Another man whose departure from the Church's ministry was surrounded with publicity (including colour supplement appearances) is the Revd Nick Stacey. An extremely gifted man, a former Olympic sprinter, Nick Stacey became a Church of England priest. After nine years as Rector of Woolwich he resigned, and is now Director of Social Services in Kent.

He remains pessimistic about the institutional Church. He thinks in its present form it will die. 'The thing is just quietly running down. The structures as we have them of full-time clergymen and lots of buildings and a large number of organisations, and the Church's role as the sort of Third Estate of the land, with the bishops in the House of Lords and the status of the hierarchy, all that has massively declined and will continue to decline.' And he does not wish to see it reviving simply because today there is a different world to minister to.

It is easy for the Churches to write off such outsiders as failures or renegades or simply unfaithful. I want to ask how far is it our fault that they are outsiders, what they have to tell us, and what we have to learn from them.

Charles Davis deliberately made himself an outsider because he believes that the official hierarchy of the Church he belonged to has taken away the right of the Christian community as a whole to decide for itself on matters of faith. The Christian community, he maintains, is kept subordinate to the bishops and archbishops, not allowed to question supposedly authoritative statements, not allowed to build up a genuine consensus of belief common to all Catholic Christians.

He decided to cut himself off from the hierarchy but not from the rest of the Catholic community. He still felt and feels in union with Catholic people, with their religious hopes and desires. Since his resignation he has found himself able to meet Roman Catholics, to take part in the celebration of the Eucharist, to be one of them. So Charles Davis remains a theologian, living the Christian life with other Christians and working for change within the Church itself. What he wants to see developing is a process of communication *upwards*, so to speak, so that the bishops, archbishops, and the Pope himself begin to express what the whole Christian community is thinking, and not simply authoritarian views.[2]

Charles Davis argues that the effects of a process of communication that is a genuine expression of freedom would not be confined simply to the Churches. There would gradually be built up a genuine consensus concerning certain political issues, which would help to counteract what he describes as 'the manipulation that takes place from above, which is destroying our present social and political life.' Although the Church must begin with issues that concern its own people, Charles Davis believes that it ought also 'to provide an example and instance of this communication and of this genuine consensus.'

Now if such a reform is needed in Roman Catholicism it could easily be needed in other Churches too. The Revd Jimmy Hamilton-Brown, the research and development officer of the Archbishop of Canterbury's Council on Evangelism, believes one is needed in the Church of England – a 'revolution', he says, which is 'going to come from the bottom and not from the top. It has got to come from the people rather than from the priests.' Jimmy Hamilton-Brown sees signs of hope particularly where Christians are starting to meet together in smaller groups than is usual in church premises, as well as in the number of lay people who are beginning to take spiritual responsibility in the churches instead of leaving it all to the clergy.

Should such developments prosper, not only might we find some genuine consensus of Christian belief on religious, social and political issues; in addition the hierarchy, in expressing this consensus, might cease to be an institutional presence with little or no support among the general public.

But supposing no consensus were reached on important issues, how would more democratic Churches cope with disagreements? Would the Christian tradition begin to disintegrate without some authority to set it out? In answer to this Charles Davis points out that the stand of the Roman Catholic Church on important issues such as apartheid has not in fact been the result of authoritative decree. Where official documents on important social and political issues have been issued, this has come after a long process of the formation of Christian consciousness and in the light of a fair degree of agreement. In any case he argues that where Christians remain in disagreement on a given point the divergence is not destructive of Christian values. 'Here', he says, 'one must be prepared to allow the tradition to struggle. Christians entering into this process must not give way to panic that the Christian tradition is going to disintegrate beyond recall.'

Could that part of the Christian Church that has remained traditionally authoritarian swallow the medicine prescribed for it by a man who still loves it but is now an outsider, then reunion with the other Churches would be much nearer. It is precisely papal and episcopal authoritarianism that the non-Roman Churches most fear, even though the other Churches have themselves a long way to go before their hierarchies learn to communicate properly with the ordinary Christian in the pews.

The Roman Catholic Church, as seen by Charles Davis, is changing. Especially in Canada and the U.S.A. he has discovered that whatever the bishops think about the authority of the Church, other Catholic Christians are starting to behave as if they have equal rights in a democratic age. Charles Davis says he has found the Catholic community 'healthier, stronger and much more flexible than I had earlier supposed.' He finds that priests and nuns as well as lay people no longer pay any attention to the declarations or commands of the bishops except when they are forced to do so. 'They themselves have, as it were, given up as regards the hierarchy.' What will happen in the end he does not know; 'whether the lower echelons of the Church will take over and absorb the higher, or whether the hierarchy will be able to bring the smaller Church under its control.'

If the Roman Catholic Church appears to be changing, what of the Church of England? When Nick Stacey resigned he did so because he felt that his Church did not want to change.

'It really was frightfully complacent,' he recalls, 'when it had absolutely no justification for complacency at all, and really rather constipated, and perhaps above all self-interested.' Nick Stacey still feels this is the case. Then as now the Church 'was terribly keen to keep the show going for the sake of the show rather than beng concerned about the Kingdom of God and changing the world and helping people.'

Nick Stacey believes that at Woolwich he was involved in exciting and promising experiments that the Church of England did not wish to take up. He was an Anglican rector, working alongside a Roman Catholic priest, a Methodist minister, a Baptist minister, a Presbyterian minister and a number of other Anglican priests who were earning their living in secular occupations. They ran a multi-purpose church, with a discotheque in the crypt, meeting rooms and offices for a housing association and the Citizens' Advice Bureau in sealed-off aisles. Nick Stacey describes it as 'a great hive of compassion and love and social activity and social concern and worship and fellowship operating from that building.' He believed they were setting a possible pattern for a church for the future; but far from being accepted as a reasonably imaginative and energetic effort, the experiments were on the whole criticised.

It is perhaps not surprising that in those days different denominations allowing their clergy to work together, a church with a discotheque in the crypt, offices in sealed-off aisles and priests in secular occupations were considered revolutionary. Since then, however, the Churches have made similar experiments with team ministries and clergy working in secular occupations. Yet Nick Stacey believes the lead given at Woolwich has not been followed in any dynamic, energetic or thrustful way. The Churches are not really concerning themselves with all the activities of men. Few worshipping communities are involved in all the daily aspects of life or even try to provide services that bring people together where the rest of the community is failing. The Church has not adopted Nick Stacey's ideals.

Perhaps there is still time for this to happen; but I must

admit that when I asked Mervyn Stockwood, who was Nick Stacey's bishop during the Woolwich experiment, how he had responded to it, I was given a rather cold reply. He told me that it was not an experiment as far as he was concerned. He had simply put into Woolwich a man with drive and imagination who did not succeed in doing all the things he would like to have done and got himself too much publicity. Mervyn Stockwood added that there are now only two persons working full-time in that particular church, which is now better attended.

Both Nick Stacey and his bishop were disappointed not to have packed Woolwich parish church with worshippers. Perhaps they wanted visible results too quickly. Dr John Robinson, who was closely involved in the experiment at Woolwich Parish Church, now sees this failure to fill the church as a valuable insight gained from Nick Stacey's work. In John Robinson's view, the experiment was 'a highly imaginative and well-run thing' which depended a great deal on Nick Stacey's personality. 'Perhaps he was (as indeed he was literally) a sprinter rather than a long distance runner and expected quick results which obviously weren't there,' is John Robinson's comment. But he thinks the work achieved much more than was probably recognised at the time. He adds that looked at as a quick-term solution to the parochial system, it did not work: Nick Stacey would be right to say, 'Do what you may, you can't really expect to fill your churches in those sort of areas in the traditional way.'

It is good that a man like John Robinson can be so warm about the Woolwich experiment. Nick Stacey may now be an outsider; but what he tried to do has great relevance for today's Churches. For instance, if the ecumenical movement is to get moving again, ministers and priests of the different British denominations ought long ago to have started working as closely together as they once did at Woolwich. And if those Churches now operating for a handful of people in some of our urban areas are to be of any real use for the Church or for the world, the ways in which Nick Stacey and his team transformed Woolwich parish church into a centre of Christian social concern surely should be followed up by others.

But the insight specially singled out by John Robinson – that neither Nick Stacey and his team nor the Churches at large seem to be able to drag into the pews ordinary working people – is not one we needed the Woolwich experiment to prove. For over 20 years the Churches' ministry to industry has worked on the assumption that by and large we do not know how to make converts of this major group in our society. The Revd Brian Cordingley, who from 1963 to 1977 was senior industrial chaplain in the diocese of Manchester, believes that many people have such a low assessment of themselves and of the things they do that the chances are they do not feel there is anything very much that they have to offer up or be thankful for or praise God about. 'I'm not simply talking about the workers of this generation,' he adds. 'It's a well-establshed statistical fact that by and large people at the lowest end, sociologically, of the working-class movement – the unskilled workers and the unskilled labourers – stopped going to church in the nineteenth century. What we have in our century is merely their successors.'[3] Not only could people living in the grinding poverty of the nineteenth century see no reason for going to church; there is also good evidence that there was not the possibility for them of going: there was not room for them and the churches did not provide for them. As a result, says Brian Cordingley, 'we now have a generation which used to go to Sunday School but has never ever gone to church.'

Nick Stacey's work (and the failure of most clergymen to achieve 'results') simply draws attention to this fact. Many people do not feel the need to thank God for their working lives because they do not set much value on their working lives. They are, as Brian Cordingley puts it, alienated. Alienation he defines as 'what happens when a person sees his creative energies as a commodity, to be sold on the market, rather than as some part of his essential being as a human person.' When people worked on the land, when people hunted, they saw survival and their work as part of their essential nature. This no longer happens in the technological world, where the selling of labour becomes normal.

This is not a peculiarly British phenomenon. Shortly before World War I the German sociologist Max Weber observed that for the modern proletariat 'the sense of dependence on one's own achievements is supplanted by a consciousness of dependence on purely social factors, market conditions, and power relationships guaranteed by law.' Weber too connected this with the observation that 'In so far as the modern proletariat has a distinctive religious position, it is characterized by indifference to and rejection of religion' (as is true, he added, of broad strata of the modern bourgeoisie).[4]

Brian Cordingley, who has spent much time studying industrial conditions abroad, believes however that for historical reasons working people in Britain are probably more alienated in this way than any other working people anywhere else in the world.

Small wonder, then, if few of them venture inside our churches. Present-day Christians ought not to blame themselves for past sins. The Churches today are not responsible for what happened in Britain in the nineteenth century. But we do in some ways aggravate the problem. Our present set-up helps to ensure that working people continue to feel themselves to be outsiders. Because in the main the clergy and ministers (especially in the Church of England) are drawn from the middle classes, we ought to be making a special effort to speak across the class barriers. But Dr Edward Norman suggests that such an effort is not being made. He describes as 'patently absurd' the new Anglican ritual which recommends that people shake hands during the service of Holy Communion. According to Edward Norman, that is something middle-class people do with great pleasure; 'it goes,' he says, 'with the sort of arts and crafts sense of things.' But, he maintains, 'for an ordinary proletarian person to go to church and start shaking hands with the bloke next door is just damn silly.'

Now I sympathize with those who are trying to 'loosen up' our worship; but it is no remedy to put in something which might not embarrass middle-class people but will only make working people feel extremely foolish. A middle-class church is in continual danger of producing worship that makes the majority of British people feel completely uncomfortable.

Professor David Martin thinks this has affected the words as well as the actions of modern forms of worship. The Churches have chosen 'to rationalize the liturgy,' he says, 'to turn it into a style that is more redolent of the businessman's office than it ever is of the office of the Church.'

I think that even businessmen, when they find themselves on their knees worshipping God, do not wish to do so in the words of their office memos! For those who neither read nor write office memos (that is, the vast majority of people in this country) the effect is only to confirm that they are outsiders. And of course they stay away. So long as our church leadership and most of our clergy are drawn from one class, the Churches will continue to express the gospel in terms that do not ring bells in the minds of working men and women. Bishop Mervyn Stockwood is perfectly clear that this is one reason why the Churches do not communicate with people who live, as he puts it, 'on the riverside'. He deplores the fact that the Church of England does not know how to train for the priesthood 'the sort of chap who becomes a Trade Union leader, but who is not the sort to read books and write essays.' As a result we have few people who can communicate with such men and women. 'As a rule it's no good sending your chaps who have a prize in Hebrew or Greek down there,' says the bishop. 'They cannot speak the language. They think differently. Their whole attitude to life is something which means very little to the people who live there.' Mervyn Stockwood is convinced that ways and means must be found of training for the priesthood those who themselves live on the riverside.

I agree with him (with the proviso that most Trade Unionists I know do actually read books). Colin Barnett, who is North West Regional Secretary of the T.U.C. and North West Divisional Officer of N.U.P.E., does not think the Churches impinge upon his work in a serious way at all. 'So often what goes on inside the Christian ghettos on a Sunday has precious little relevance to what goes on in the world outside,' he says. It therefore has little relevance for his life as a Trade Union official. And he feels that because the Churches are relatively cosy communities, people often withdraw into them to avoid facing up to the real issues which others have to face every day.

Of course such congregations might well defeat some of those clergymen who want the Churches to change. Colin Barnett accuses many lay members of the Churches of being intellectually 'particularly idle'. Those who are not, he wants to stay within the Church and work out a proper strategy with the clergy, who, he observes, 'sometimes hide behind their own professionalism and are not prepared to argue out with the laity the doubts and concerns they obviously have.' Unless this happens within the next ten years Colin Barnett expects the Churches to become increasingly moribund and irrelevant.

His view is reinforced by the Revd Jimmy Hamilton-Brown, who says that until we get some sort of effective Christian leadership out of the ordinary church member we shall not get very far at all. He thinks 'the whole clue lies in something to do with leadership, and clergy being prepared to spend a lot of time with a small number of people, where they are and where they work.' Many church members, he believes, are perfectly capable of leading groups. Since leadership is a gift of the Holy Spirit, our faith should lead us to expect to find in our congregations people capable of exercising that gift. But he warns that it will not be just one type of leadership, 'not all the educated middle-class variety of leadership. In some parishes you will have a completely different type of leadership.'

We are at present a long way off that goal, but it might just happen: leadership in the Churches exercised by the men and women in the pews. Until we take that demand seriously, many will remain outsiders who should be inside. It will involve the kind of revolution upwards envisaged by Charles Davis, as well as some of the patterns of leadership in industry and the Trade Unions that the Churches have not yet cottoned on to. We need to foster that kind of democracy in our churches. Perhaps more clergy working in secular occupations, such as those mentioned by Nick Stacey, could help to show us a way. And certainly the experiments like the one at Woolwich should be looked at again as possible patterns of work and worship and service in some of our almost redundant church buildings.

The outsiders have a lot more to teach us than I expected when I began this research. Yet so much still depends on the attitude, the quality and the roles of the clergy. They can either encourage or hamper the movements of the Spirit among lay people. They can try to learn from the outsiders, or they can retreat into their cosy ghettos and allow the Churches to die. They can make courageous experiments or remain cautiously irrelevant.

We need to investigate what is happening to the clergy. How are they being trained? Are the theological colleges training students for tomorrow's ministry or for yesterday's? Have the Churches through the clergy any real ministry to industry? What of those men who are working as priests in secular occupations? And since a good half of the people in the pews are women, do the Christian Churches yet know how to use *their* ministry and talents?

1. Charles Davis *A Question of Conscience*, Hodder and Stoughton paperback edition 1969, p. 16.
2. On this see E. J. Yarnold, S. J. and Henry Chadwick *Truth and Authority, A Commentary on the Agreed Statement of the Anglican-Roman Catholic International Commission, Venice 1976*, C.T.S./S.P.C.K. 1977, especially pp. 20ff., 27 and 29f.
3. See E. R. Wickham *Church and People in an Industrial Society*, Lutterworth Press 1956, for an historical analysis of this phenomenon.
4. M. Weber *Economy and Society*, Totowa and Bedminster 1968, p. 486.

[5]
Onward Christian Soldiers!

The Revd Jack Burton drives a bus in Norwich. He is also an ordained Methodist minister and for five years ran his own Methodist church.

He took up bus driving out of a deep sense of isolation. Before doing so he felt, he says, that he had been shunted into a siding while the main line trains raced by. 'I was uninvolved,' he says, 'and I knew that I had to have the world as well as the Church.' So in 1968 he put in an application to the Methodist Church authorities to earn his own living in a way that would bring him into daily contact with the people who ignored all the welcome notices he put up outside the church. Since then he has been working as a busman, continuing nevertheless to preach, celebrate the sacraments, visit the sick and generally do all those things he believes he was called, trained and ordained to do.

If it is surprising to find a minister driving a bus, that shows how few experiments the Christian Churches have made in the ministry over the last 20 years. Many other parsons must have felt as isolated as Jack Burton was. Many must have put up notices outside church which nobody noticed. Yet while huge sections of the population of Britain never look inside a church door, the clergy for the most part have been encouraged to carry on in the old ways, faithfully doing the same old things, watching their congregations dwindle away.

Of course what Jack Burton did is in a sense a criticism of the Church as it now exists. To enter the full-time ministry, to feel called to serve a church full-time, and then to say one feels uninvolved in real life sounds threatening. Not surprisingly Jack Burton found permission to change hard to get. 'At one stage,' he says, 'it was a question of sort of stand-up rows, all very unseemly' Permission was originally given for three years. At the end of those three years he was asked if he would like to carry on; and that is more or less the last he has heard about it. Most years he receives a hint that the experiment might be stopped; but he is still driving his bus and he senses far more sympathy now from the church authorities than he did in 1968.

That sympathy could suggest that the Methodist Church is becoming aware of the need for a much more dynamic and missionary ministry if clergymen are not to go on preaching a redundant gospel to empty churches. Most churches in Britain are cautious bodies. One man in the leadership of the Church of England who has responded to the Church's problems by experimenting did so under the banner of caution. When Mervyn Stockwood was made Bishop of Southwark in 1959 his sermon announced 'a cautious experiment with regard to the training of ordination candidates and their subsequent employment.' His ideas were at the time extremely startling. Instead of training future clergymen in a theological college, he started the Southwark Ordination Course, using residential week-end and summer schools. The Extra-Mural Department of London University provided the academic resources. And most startling of all, the Course did not expect all its men to give up their ordinary work once they put on clerical collars. After five years only half of those ordained had become full-time clergy; the other half were the Jack Burtons of the Church of England, without his trauma of starting a full-time ministry and having to get out again.

Mervyn Stockwood's right-hand man at this time was Dr John Robinson. Looking back today he describes the Southwark Ordination Course as 'one of the few things that has really taken off.' He thinks it is stronger today than it ever has been.

John Robinson describes the Course as 'a sort of do-it-yourself theological college without walls.' Instead of taking people *out of* the world to train them for ministry *to* the world, it presupposed that they would continue at work and supporting their own families. No-one was required to decide before the course started whether or not they would give up their work afterwards and go into the full-time parochial ministry. In the early days the majority did. Now, says John Robinson, the majority does not. This change is hardly surprising. In view of the financial problems facing the Churches (and indeed every large employer with dwindling assets) more people will find it easier to earn a living doing another job rather than working as a full-time parson.

But this 'auxiliary ministry', as people call it, cannot simply solve some of the problems involved in paying the clergy – and especially the married clergy – a living wage without affecting much else in the Churches as we have come to know them. What will be the effect on congregations of clergymen who are not there all the time? Will it weaken the Churches? Mervyn Stockwood, who is the only man with any long-term managerial experience of the scheme, does not think so. He told me of a small village in the southern part of his diocese. In spite of its lovely old village church, the diocese could not afford to let the villagers have a priest. But a man who works in the city is ordained and lives in the rectory. He receives no stipend, but on Sundays he celebrates the Holy Communion and he is available in so far as he has time during the week. 'The church has come to life,' says Mervyn Stockwood, 'in a most encouraging way. Now it is the laity who visit the sick and bereaved, and who help the people preparing for baptism and confirmation.'

If that is the case, it is possible that this 'auxiliary' part time ministry might not only solve some financial problems for the Churches. It might also help to bring about something much more important: the desctruction of the notion that the real Christians are the clergy and that the laity just help them. This Southwark scheme has been taken up with some modifications in many other parts of the Church of England: in the East Midlands, in the North West, in the diocese of St Albans for example.[1] But wherever part-time priests begin to work, new thinking by them and their congregations is called for. The expectations of the laity must change. Many have believed in the past (and still believe) that a priest or minister is different from themselves. If he goes wrong the whole system is threatened.

Upon his gifts or lack of them depends almost everything. Yet the priesthood of all believers means that anyone who becomes a Christian is set apart. Is the fundamental reason for an ordained professional ministry primarily to celebrate the sacraments? Has the priest a further role in preaching and teaching, to educate his fellow Christians in the faith, in humanity and growth? May we see in these theological colleges without walls laymen and women training themselves as Christians *alongside* ordinands and clergymen? May we once again begin to see that to be a clergyman is not so much to have a profession as a vocation?

In spite of these questions the foreseeable future will still see at least some full-time clergy. And at present most theological colleges are still run on more traditional lines than the Southwark Course and its successors. Yet these traditional colleges are asking the same questions. The principal of St John's College, Nottingham, the Revd Robin Nixon, believes that the people of God in a given area, that is those Christians who actually live and work there, are basically responsible to God for the work of the Church in that place. The clergy are there essentially to help them. 'So often in the past,' he says, 'people have thought: "The Vicar is there. He's responsible, and we're going to help him. We'll give him a bit of help here and a bit of help there. We're really being very decent and nice about it." But in the end they don't feel they have a responsibility to God.'

Robin Nixon believes that attitude must change; and his college trains ordinands in that belief. But most of our congregations are probably still a long way from his ideal, still looking to the parson to be the real Christian, with themselves as auxiliaries.

And I have a fear that the protective atmosphere of our traditional enclosed theological colleges might be concealing from some of the ordinands the cruel realities outside. Robin Nixon allowed me to talk with some of his students about the awesome financial problems facing the churches. One told me he was not particularly worried if his future parishes were unable or unwilling to pay him a living wage. 'I really do think things will work out on that score,' he said. 'It's amazing at College here how money turns up when people are in need. People are wanting to come and do a course who set out with no money at all, and it does arrive.'

One could call that faith, or one could call it naivety. I was relieved that Robin Nixon is deeply conscious of the dangers in throwing people unprepared into the harsh world when they have been cocooned in College for three years or more. He told me that there have been occasions when people have gone out expecting to find things outside as they found them in the College, and then been terribly disillusioned.

It became clear to me as I talked with the ordinands that those who intend to work as full-time parish priests have no intention of perpetuating the old notion of the one-type soldier army with the parson doing everything. One student had given up a successful business career to come into the full-time ministry precisely when the Churches are facing a recession. He believes his business experience will help him to change the way most parsons still work. As a relatively inexperienced young man his managing director sent him abroad simply to try and sell the firm's goods. Although the managing director hugely enjoyed that kind of work himself, he had the gift of delegation. That gift is needed in the churches if we are to destroy what this student called 'the old pyramid system, where you have the vicar at the top with a finger in every pie.' For, as he said, within the body of Christ every Christian is called to continue Christ's ministry on earth in the power of the Spirit.

Such neat and encouraging blends of business acumen and Christian theology are clearly stimulated by the College vice-principal, the Revd Colin Buchanan, who encourages his students to jettison the obsolete patterns of yesterday's ministry. He says he does not want them to get the feeling he was given as an ordinand: that the Church of England, its graveyards and its buildings, remain unchanging, all going back hundreds of years and destined to go on for hundreds of years, upheld by a clergy patterned in the same unchanging mould.

Colin Buchanan has made a detailed study of the job prospects of Anglican clergymen.[2] The picture he paints is one of Church leaders encouraging men to offer themselves for the full-time ministry, lamenting the fact that fewer and fewer are coming forward, but never stopping to ask how many jobs are actually going to be available. That confusion was high-lighted at the beginning of 1977, when the Archbishop of Canterbury sent a letter to every Anglican parish priest saying that the Church of England in the 1980s will face a grave manpower shortage unless the decline in men coming forward for the full-time ministry can be halted. At precisely the same moment the Association of Clergy was complaining, in a letter to every member of the church's General Synod, because the Church of England cannot adequately pay the men it has already got.[3]

Just how many full-time clergymen can the Churches afford? Colin Buchanan is not certain that there will be jobs for all the men in training now. He believes that there will always be a job 'for the man who has some ability to have a bird's-eye view of what he is doing, to see where the resources have to be put into the church, to bring an understanding of the truth of God to the particular people who are leaders (though *they* may be people doing other jobs).' But he is anxious about those men 'who are not particularly noticeable.'

I wonder how many there are who are 'not particularly noticeable'. Certainly the churches cannot carry such people today. The clergy can no longer simply coast along, in a cosy and safe world called the Church. If this is a grim fact, it is good that it is being recognised. And it is good, too, to find some church leaders acknowledging that for too long we have been working with a wrong understanding of the role of the man and woman in the pew. Archbishop Derek Worlock believes that 'as the laity enter fully into their own proper position in the life of the Church, the role of the priest as the spiritual caller, animator, leader of worship, will become clearer. He has got to call. He has got to sustain. He has got to help people who are equally doing God's work in their own particular spheres.'

What worries me is whether the people in the pews recognise

this themselves. Have the old ways so stifled lay initiative that those who might have taken the lead in waking up our Churches have simply walked out, abandoning them to those who simply want to leave everything to the vicar? I cannot forget the Revd Jack Burton, feeling himself shunted onto a side-line whilst the main line trains passed him and his church by. Jack Burton admits he has found a kind of honesty and openness outside the Church that he never knew inside. For him 'it's the very breath of life compared with the deference which is traditionally shown inside church to clergymen.' He feels he can be himself at work in a way in which he would hesitate to be in church. To him this seems all wrong. It ought in theory to be the other way round 'In the loving community,' he says, 'one ought to be able to relax; but in fact the barriers which we put up between ourselves are as secure in the Church as in the world, and indeed, I'm tempted to think, even more so.'

To find the breath of life outside rather than inside church; to find barriers between people inside church securer than those outside; these might be written off as simply one man's reactions, were they not confirmed by the testimony of other people. Charles Davis no longer thinks the Churches need a full-time priesthood (though they may need a small number of full time ministers). He now believes that it is 'better from the point of view of the priest – his relationship with the congregation and his own sense of identity – that he should have some other job besides his priesthood, but that he should exercise a priestly ministry to a small group.'

So the full-time ministry can spoil a man's relationship with his congregation and warp his sense of identity, whereas taking up a secular job can allow a clergyman to be himself again. It also enables him to be more involved in the world. The second Vatican Council deliberated a great deal about involvement in the world. Priests as laity were to live in the real circumstances of life rather than in the withdrawn life of the presbytery. One of the ways in which Charles Davis became involved in life outside the presbytery, so to speak, was by marrying. He believes that vocation to celibacy and vocation to the priesthood should not be brought together in an inseparable fashion, as in the Roman Catholic Church. They are two separable vocations, he says, and a person who has a priestly vocation does not necessarily have a vocation to celibacy.

If Roman Catholic clergy are to express the faith in a way that fits in with real life, it seems to me that some of them at any rate ought to be allowed to break down a barrier between themselves and most other people by getting to understand what it means to be married. But the Archbishop of Liverpool did not agree with me when I put that to him. He believes that not being married makes it easier for him to help those who are. His experience as a priest, he says, 'is that many many married people have turned to me for counsel, not only with the knowledge that I'm not married but with the realisation that my celibacy has cost me something, and that it is sign – a most meaningful sign at the present moment and in these times – of my total dedication.'

Whatever new patterns of ministry emerge in the Roman Catholic Church, this particular barrier between priest and people seems likely to remain, at least for the time being. The Church of England more or less takes Charles Davis's line, namely that some people are called to marry and some are not, but that has nothing to do with whether you are going to be a priest or not.

The Church of England is agonizing over another attempt to break down the barriers between the clergy and everyone else. Dare the Church of England ordain women priests? Already other parts of the world-wide Anglican communion have ordained women, leaving their old mother Church of England behind. A majority in the Church thinks there are no theological objections to ordaining women, but the decision to do so has been postponed for an indefinite period. But in the coming few years there will be about 50 women priests in the American Episcopal Church, to give one example of what is happening elsewhere.

In the Church of England there are about 80 women who

want to be ordained. Why shouldn't they be? For a 100 years women have served in other professions, for example as doctors and lawyers, with dignity and distinction. A girl studying at Nottingham Theological College gave me two reasons against ordaining them, one social, the other taken from St. Paul. 'Quite apart from our cultural background,' she said, 'I don't really see women fitting into that role. The way I understand Paul's writing on it is that women are not to have spiritual authority over men. That seems to me quite plain and simple, and I'm willing to abide by it.'

When I put these two points to Bishop Mervyn Stockwood, who stands on the Catholic wing of the Church of England, he pointed out that not only have social conditions changed; so has our understanding of St Paul. 'After all, the governor of our Church is a woman, the Queen,' he observed; 'and if you can have a woman who is the supreme governor of the Church of England, and a woman who is the leader of one of the largest political parties in the country,[4] well, I think that the time may come when we might have women priests.' St Paul, he said, 'was a man of his age.' Women in that position in Paul's time would be a very different thing from women being ordained today. (Mervyn Stockwood added that St Paul said quite a few things that all Christians do not necessarily accept. He says that even he, as a bachelor, is not willing to go along with the low view of marriage implied in the apostle's dictum that it is better to marry than to burn!)

To the articulate opposition provoked by the imminent prospect of ordaining women, leaders of the movement to ordain them, such as Una Kroll, have become equally articulate in reply. They see as the principle objection that Christianity is a partriarchal religion, with male images of God, as Father, Son and Holy Spirit. Moreover, God became incarnate as a man (in whose priesthood the ordained share) and he appointed no women to be his apostles.

Una Kroll says that if Christiantiy does worship a male God there is no place in that religion for women. She believes, however, that the witness of the first book of the Bible (in which God is said to have created both men and women in his own image) implies that within the Godhead can be seen all that is perfectly female as well as all that is perfectly male. Although our theology has in her opinion become terribly twisted by the way we always refer to God as Father and refuse to think of Christ in terms of a mother, she draws attention to theologians, including notably Julian of Norwich, who have recognised the feminine element within the Godhead. She also say that there is 'a beyondness within the Godhead which surmounts male and female.'

For these reasons Una Kroll remains in the Church. Because Churches are not institutions that easily accept radical change, she is aware that the step of ordaining women divides and even causes church members to leave. She believes that the importance of ordaining women outweighs these disadvantages. For her the symbolic value of ordaining even a few women will not only set out the full imagery of the Godhead; saying that women can represent God as fully as men can represent God will also lead women outside the Churches to think of themselves in terms of deep value. And the partnership between men and women, which now exists but needs to be more fully expressed, will, she believes, become a greater reality.

Una Kroll does not suppose that women priests will simply supplement the ministry of men as priests. 'All the evidence I have,' she says, 'points to the fact that women have a different dimension to offer. Therefore the priesthood will change. And men will be able to express what they are without having to think about including the feminine.' Lastly, Una Kroll believes that in such a situation the participation of the laity will change as well.

If those are the fruits of ordaining women, then we ought to have ordained them long ago. Ordaining women priests will not instantly persuade more people to come into the Churches. Radical steps of this kind tend to make some people leave. But the point of ordaining women priests is not to fill the pews but to make the Churches better servants of the Kingdom of God: to enhance the world as well as the Churches; to improve people's understanding of God; to help lay Christians to become more conscious of their own vocation.

I found these elements when I looked at the Churches' ministry to industry. In Britain today there are about 150 full-time industrial chaplains, helped by about the same number doing the work part-time. Drawn from all the major denominations, they visit various industrial plants up and down the country, concerned to get to know well those who work there, to join in their life, perhaps in the way the old village parson came to know his parishioners in the days before industrialisation. One of their hopes is to provide opportunities for people on opposite sides of all kinds of fences (but particularly the management-worker fence) to meet one another as human beings and discuss what affects their lives.

The Revd Brian Cordingley says 'it's not the aim of industrial mission at this stage to get more people simply to come to church.' As Urban and Industrial Missioner for the Bishop of Manchester he is prepared to go along with all kinds of people who want to think through in some depth what their faith and beliefs might mean in terms of their work, their political life, their learning and educational life, their citizenship.

Brian Cordingley is not entirely sure that the institutional Churches as they are at the moment are completely committed to doing that themselves. It seems to me that the Churches need industrial chaplains, and indeed all Christians who are willing to risk living deep inside the secular world, as researchers, feeding back into the Churches information about that world,[5] as well as taking with them into that world the resources of the Christian tradition.

The three elements of the Christian faith which Brian Cordingley singles out as vital and clearly seen in the person of Jesus Christ are faith, compassion and relevance in the world. We have to look around and find out where these three elements are present. 'Wherever faith, compassion and relevance come together, we ought to be nurturing and nourishing these movements,' he says. 'Wherever institutions are willing to nurture these movements, we should encourage the institutions.

Wherever institutions are obstacles and obstructions to these movements, then we must fight against the institutions, so that these signs of the Kingdom can in fact grow and become the Church of the future.'

That sums up the task of all the patterns of ministry I have been examining, and also gives criteria for judging them. The Christian faith and the compassion that flows from it remain the same: but the Churches must show their relevance in a continually changing world, a task which is clearly demanding new forms of ministry. But it is not simply a matter of clergy taking up and developing this ministry. The Christians in the pews must encourage and support them in this. The men and women in the pews can no longer expect their clergy to do everything for them in the Churches. Unless they release clergy for new patterns of ministry and with them work out strategies for mission, the Churches will remain mostly irrelevant to the modern world. Lay Christians, therefore, must stand on their own feet. But will they?

1. More information from A.C.C.M., Church House, Dean's Yard, London SW1.
2. C. Buchanan *Inflation, Deployment and the Job Prospects of the Clergy*, Grove Books, Nottingham, 1976.
3. *The Guardian*, 1 February 1977, p.7, reports both letters in the same columns.
4. Mrs Margaret Thatcher.
5. Chapter 6, 'The mission of the Church in an industrial society', of E. R. Wickham *Church and People in an Industrial Society*, is a pioneering piece of research of this kind. Its insights need supplementing in the light of the experience of industrial mission since that book was written.

[6]
Death and Resurrection

'Were in a situation where the new Church is somewhere around in the old institution and on its fringes, but not yet clearly visible and emerging.' This comment from the Revd Brian Cordingley, after 20 years' work in industrial mission, offers hope. Yet as this book has shown, however you look at the facts, from whatever point of view, most Churches in Britain today are in trouble. Fewer and fewer people bother to worship inside their buildings. Fewer men offer themselves for the full-time ministry (though minor fluctuations in the numbers coming forward allow church leaders still to speculate that things might get better).

Where, then, is this new Church to be found? Can we identify any signs of new life in the search for the Kingdom of God? Dr Colin Morris insists that Churches are not so much structures as organisms, in which all the time 'some cells are dying while other cells are growing'. So he can admit that in some areas of Britain the Churches are dead. And according to Professor David Martin, Christians ought not to be over-despondent about this, for in his view the Churches have always been in the course of some kind of destruction in order to find resurrection.

The famous sociologist Ernst Troeltsch believed that where traditional religious institutions lose their influence in an urban environment 'they are replaced by a more flexible and individualistic form of religion rather than by none at all.'[1] There is evidence that the spirituality and idealism of such new patterns of Christian faith can be utilised and supported by equally flexible structures. One such structure is the Christian Education Movement. It employs a dozen full-time and 20 part-time staff (who include only three clergymen), working in schools and in more informal spheres with young persons, offering a Christian critique of the whole of education as well as guidance in religious education. About 2,000 secondary schools and 1300 primary schools throughout Britain are associated with the movement. Over 2,000 personal members of the movement – clergymen, teachers, parents – receive its publications regularly (*Learning for Living*, issued to all members, *Common Room* for secondary teachers, and *Primary Response* for primary teachers).[2]

Another enlightening response to the facts of the situation today is provided by the Institute of Religion and Medicine. (For the Institute 'religion' implies any creed, but in this country means chiefly Christianity.) Financed entirely by voluntary subscription, the Institute has a membership of some 1200 doctors, nurses, social workers, clergymen, occupational therapists, psychiatrists and people drawn from other professions concerned with health care. It sponsors 40 British field groups, which involve very many who are not formal members. Each has a local secretary. Some meet in houses, some in hospitals. Sometimes the members listen to an outside speaker; at other times they pursue a theme in group discussion, relying solely on their own resources. The Institute runs an annual three-day conference, a day conference in London and similar ones in the provinces.[3]

Occasionally its publications reach wider notice[4]; but its influence works chiefly through the infiltration of ideas by means of the study notes circulated regularly to members, and by the inspiration that comes from men and women in related disciplines who meet to look at the deeper implications of their work and their faith.

These groups (and there are others like them) flourish alongside but also outside our traditional church structures. (Some groups, like the Church of England's Board for Social Responsibility[5], try to do the same thing from within a traditional church structure.) They recognize a diffuse religious commitment which the Churches in their present form seem no longer to be able to sustain or deploy.

No body has been able to engage this commitment more dramatically than Christian Aid.[6] The one and a quarter million pounds it raised in Britain in 1966 had become an annual total of nearly £5 million ten years later. Janet Lacey, who ran Christian Aid until her retirement in 1968, wrote that 'a significant feature of society today is the fact that the Churches together have done, and are doing, more for suffering humanity than almost any other institution and this is true to their calling.' She added: 'even more significant is the increasing compulsion of ordinary men and women, including young people, living in an increasingly sophisticated world, who while unable to accept the Christian faith in a "package deal" or as a philosophy of life, are in large numbers occupied with caring for the refugees, the persecuted, the homeless and all in need.' To challenge and make use of this compulsion is part of the work of Christian Aid.

Its success argues for Christian unity. As Janet Lacey writes, 'surely united action for the hungry world is an essential manifestation of the teaching of Jesus.' The success of Christian Aid also calls for changes in the life and work of the Churches in order to meet the demands of the present day. The stubborn resistance to such changes, says Janet Lacey, 'may well ultimately kill the Church as we know it.'[7] Yet those clergymen who have spent all their working lives trying to keep the old Churches going, and those lay Christians who have worked sacrificially in the same cause, find it hard to contemplate such changes, for they themselves would constitute the death of much that they have invested their emotional lives in.

For this reason, perhaps, Dr Andrew Ross finds many in the Church of Scotland arguing that they are not really in a crisis. In fact the Church of Scotland has made by far the most systematic attempt of all the institutional Churches to repond to some of today's problems. Having commissioned the department of economics at Edinburgh University to examine its finances, the Church set up a Committee of Forty (convened by Professor Robin Barbour of Aberdeen University) to recommend ways of reorganisation.

The committee believes that although from many angles the future for institutional Christianity in Scotland looks dark, 'this is not a time for foreboding; it is a time of hope, provided that we can make the drastic changes in our attitudes and in our institutions that God calls us to make.' It wants the church to set up 'community parishes' which cut across obsolete denominational and parochial boundaries. It wants to look realistically at the use of buildings. It wants stronger Christian communities to look how they can help weaker ones. Above all the committee stresses the strength that is derived from working in small groups.

In spite of the steady decrease in membership of the Church of Scotland over the past 15 years, the number of its elders (that is, its lay leaders) stands at 48,000 – higher than ever before. The committee wants these men and women to play a much greater part in the life and councils of the Church. To allow this to happen, the difference between the ordained and lay ministry must be drastically reduced.[8] And, the committee stresses, men and women in the Church must be trained for leadership. 'Let there be no doubt about it, effective small groups do not just happen. They need the unobtrusive support and skill of trained leadership in the area.'[9]

Whether or not the Church of Scotland will respond to these recommendations remains to be seen. But I agree with Dr Andrew Ross when he deplores the notion that 'if we just streamline here, re-jig there, everything will be all right.' That he regards as 'the recipe for death'; and death, I would think, without the possibility of resurrection.

Those who remain inside the institutional Churches need to learn from those who have walked out while still remaining Christians. Nick Stacey does not think the Churches will disappear; but he sees their pattern as being 'much more along the lines of the Quaker movement, a pattern in which people will meet in small groups and break bread and have fellowship and prayer, and discuss and work out action they can take to build up the Kingdom of God.' What he does not envisage surviving is what he describes as 'this massive great super-structure – buildings and full-time agents and the whole sort of razamataz – which is now of course out of all proportion to the grass-roots support it has.'

Although Nick Stacey's dislike of the structures of the Church seems at times diffused and unspecific, so that it is not easy to say what he would destroy, the vision of what he would keep is clear enough. Such a pattern of Christian life would involve the death of much of what we have come to regard as essential to Christianity in our land. But nothing shows more clearly the soul-destroying aimlessness of much present-day Christian activity than the way dwindling bands of the faithful are expected to devote much of their time to propping up redundant church buildings at the expense of everything else. As an Anglican layman as well as a Trade Union officer Colin Barnett has come to believe that a building in some ways holds back Christian advance today. It holds back Christian commitment and inhibits a proper Christian presence in the world. 'We have to spend all our time worrying how we are going to pay for the fuel bills, worrying how we are going to keep this institution going which is probably far too big for our needs.' He believes Christians would be far more effective if they simply met in each others' houses most of the time, coming together on occasions in church buildings for major services. 'I would not cry my eyes out,' he says, 'to see a great many churches closed down completely.'

Nor would I. There is little problem in getting people to pay for the upkeep of beautiful historic buildings that have some significance for the community (though for too long many such churches have failed to make use of the resources of responsible professional fund-raisers to do this); but to throw onto the backs of dedicated clergymen and laymen the burden of keeping dry-rot out of useless piles of bricks and mortar has nothing to do with Christianity.

To demolish architecturally valuable buildings simply because in their present state they seem no longer useful to the furtherance of Christianity is vandalism. But fresh uses can be found for them. St Thomas's, Southgate Street, 'the most ambitious Victorian Church in Winchester,'[10] today fittingly house the Hampshire Record Office. In London Holy Trinity, Marylebone Road, built by Sir John Soane in 1825, is occupied by a publisher of religious books, and St John, Smith Square, has been restored as a cultural centre. St Peter, Hungate, in Norwich, is now a diocesan museum. And the medieval church which enhances the beautiful market place of Richmond, Yorkshire, is in fact no longer a church but discreetly embodies offices and shops.

Unless more such uses are found, a good number of clergymen will find themselves becoming what Bryan Wilson alleges others already are: little more than 'custodians of tourist shrines.' To free parishoners from the burdens of such buildings will release Christian energies, will bring together congregations to do the real work of building up the Kingdom of God, and might even provide a bit more money to pay some full-time clergy a decent wage. As we begin to see redundant church buildings disappearing or being put into better use, that will be a sign of life!

Of course one reason why we have so many church buildings in spite of empty pews is that Britain has inherited so many different Christian denominations. After years of the ecumenical movement the denominations are still running rival shows, competing for a dwindling public. The failure of the denominations fully to accept each other as Christians must appear to outsiders as a total denial of the gospel that these same denominations are supposed to preach. Yet the movement towards unity seems almost dead, even though, as the Rt Revd Patrick Rodger (who was chairman of the Churches' Unity Commission for England) observes, the basic question in our present society is just how does one live as a Christian 'and only very secondarily as an Anglican or as a Methodist, or a Roman Catholic, or a Baptist.'

A former priest of the Episcopal Church of Scotland, Patrick Rodger is now Bishop of Oxford. For five years in the early 1960s he ran extremely successfully the Faith and Order section of the World Council of Churches in Geneva. Since then, he believes, the further decline of the institutional churches and the secularisation of the countries of the west have produced in Christians here 'a certain kind of defensiveness, a kind of "what we have we hold" attitude, which doesn't always make people braver in going forward.'

Dwindling numbers ought to make Christians realise that they are all active partners in mission and service of the world. Since, according to Patrick Rodger, this has not happened, it is barely surprising that in 1972, when the Church of England and the Methodist Church were about to re-unite, the General Synod of the Church of England at the last minute could not muster a big enough majority to go ahead.

There is, however, more to that failure than mere Christian fearfulness in a secular age. Many who desire Christian unity do not want a mammoth uniform Church as its manifestation. In so far as this is what the Anglicans and Methodists were heading for in 1972, they were perhaps misled at the time. That pattern of Christian unity is better dead.

However, the failure to unite in 1972 raised a much more important problem, common to many British Churches. Re-union between Anglicans and Methodists in England would have gone through whatever the members of the General Synod thought, if enough lay Christians had wanted it. What in fact happened is that the leaders of the two Churches worked out a deal which they then expected to filter downwards; they were not really responding to pressure upwards, to pressure from the lay members of both Churches.

Has anything been learned since then? Did the new Churches' Unity Commission for England plan to produce agreements and perhaps even schemes of re-union with next-to-no consultation with lay opinion? Patrick Rodger claims that the members of the Commission desired to 'plug in' to any lay impetus towards unity they could find. But when asked how many laymen serve on the Commission, he frankly admitted that 'officially it's not very lay. We do have lay members, and some very good and active ones in the work of our Commission; but there's no blinking the fact that it's primarily clerical.'

Here then was a Commission set up by eight participating Churches in the old predominantly clerical way, at a time when there were nearly 300 local ecumenical projects in England alone, sharing buildings, sharing ministers, sharing congregational life and worship, and sharing decision-making.[11] Very many lay persons are actively engaged in these projects. They should be 'officially' involved in the Churches' moves towards unity.

The fact that they are not is symptomatic of the whole topsy-turvy structure of many Churches. Dr Edward Norman believes that this is getting worse in the Church of England. He deplores the 'large, seemingly growing secretariat at Church House, producing a volume of reports for the very top-heavy structures of synodical government.' He sees this happening across the whole Church, where proliferating committees are producing a bureaucratic structure that is weakening the voice of the Church. Its leadership, he believes, 'has been too much absorbed by bureaucratised responses,' as a result, 'so we get a sort of public relations voice beginning to be spoken by the bishops themselves.' (Edward Norman adds that there is 'not enough ordinary straightforward vulgarity' on the bishop's bench; 'it's all far too nice.')

It is a sign of hope when the bureaucratic structures of the Churches are challenged in this way. That criticism should ally itself with the growing demand from some lay men and women for a real voice in church affairs. Our present structures stop the voice of the ordinary man and woman in the pews being heard. The in-built dominance of the clergy encourages lay people in the disastrous belief that they are only the second-class Christians. It means that the statements of the hierarchy are often out-of-touch with what ordinary Christians are thinking. As Charles Davis expresses the situation, 'Where you have a structure which is built on a hierarchical order of authority, with power firmly above and structure in terms of domination from above, then a genuine consensus is rendered impossible.' He believes that 'this has been made very clear in the Catholic Church on key issues concerning, for example, birth control, where the formation of a genuine consensus has been blocked by an exercise of hierarchical authority.'

The Churches will never get any effective leadership from the laity until they are rid of that kind of structure, until the hierarchy (including perhaps her the humbler clergy too) relinquishes its stranglehold on everything important and dies in its present form, so that the voice of the average Christian in this land can be heard.

For this reason good may emerge from the steep decline in the numbers of clergymen, if it makes the Churches start taking their lay members seriously. Jimmy Hamilton-Brown states quite baldly that we need 'far less clergy, and far more laity actually doing things and saying things and being leaders in the Church.' Similarly Archbishop Derek Worlock, though concerned about the decline in the number of Roman Catholic priests in Britain, says that even though there are fewer priests, there are more people actively engaged in the life of the Church. 'If we are relying entirely on priests,' he says, 'the diminution in the number of priests means the diminution in the activity of the church. If we are seeing the priest's role as being the leadership of his people, and that the people are the Church and are doing the work of the church, then there are more people engaged in that work than before.'

The perceptible shift in clerical attitudes displayed here becomes even more marked where members of what is still sometimes called the 'auxiliary' ministry, part-time priests of good theological training, lead the worship of God in the local congregation but earn their living doing a job elsewhere. In some parts of Britain this has led to lay men and women being given by the church spiritual responsibilities in visiting the sick and helping the bereaved. They can no longer leave things to the parson. They and he together have to work out what is necessary to serve the Kingdom of God in the places where they live and work. And these part-time clergymen find that as the old pattern dies they have a better relationship with their congregations and a securer sense of their own identity if they too are immersed for their livelihood in the secular world.

Here may be developing in some Churches a new sort of responsible democracy. This is one reason why the Churches should welcome the points at which the insights of the Pentecostal Churches are spilling over into our more traditional Christian bodies. The Pentecostal belief that the Holy Spirit can and should speak through anyone in church, not just through those who wear clerical collars, might give a powerful impetus towards much more democratic Church structures and patterns of lay participation.

Such possibilities should make us more ready to accept the break-up of our existing denominational structures. For too long the various denominations, feeling strong enough to go it alone, have been able to ignore each other for most purposes. Perhaps now they can start to learn from each other and thus improve the ways in which they serve the world outside. Unity amongst Christians would decisively affect our understanding of the unity of mankind.[12] Patrick Rodger illuminated this for me, when he confessed to being puzzled by the failure of the Anglican-Methodist reunion scheme, but added, 'I think class had quite a lot to do with it, quite frankly.' The class system that divides Britain helps to divide our Churches. In Britain only a united Church might have a membership that crosses these class barriers.

Christian unity is needed soon. It outght not to be put off till some time in the next century or the one after that. Above all I would like to see brought into the Anglican and Protestant Churches in Britain the experiences of those who make up the membership of the Roman Catholic Church here. I recognize that this cannot happen until the Roman Catholic hierarchy begins to understand its role in a much more democratic fashion, as representing the collective views of the whole Christian community.

This prescription naturally means the death of our different denominations (though not of different patterns of worship and ministry). But if they die, each Christian will be immeasurably enriched by the traditions from which he is at the moment cut off. The more spiritually aware a man becomes, the more conscious he is of the limitations of his own worship and his need for such enrichment.

And the most disparate Christian bodies have much to teach each other. Fr Simon Tugwell thinks that the Pentecostal Churches, because they have rediscovered some of the basic human roots underlying all religious experience, have much to teach his own Roman Catholic Church, which he says has come close to setting up a supernatural sacramental structure without anything to stand on.

In my view Roman Catholics are not alone in needing to rediscover the natural roots underlying all religious experience. All our principal Churches have been so keen to keep up with the trends of our secularised society that they have almost forgotten many of the religious symbols that lie in the collective unconscious – symbols of fire and wind and cleansing, for instance. Professor David Martin argues that because the Churches are ceasing to respond to these symbols, their vitality is in danger of being transferred elsewhere, for example into all kinds of hidden-wisdom cults and eastern cults. Some of the Christian symbols of hope and solidarity and faith have, he believes, been revived in political contexts. So because we are losing touch with the roots of our religion, its strengths start operating elsewhere; others are gaining at our expense. The reckless way in which liturgical experiment has jettisoned traditional religious language is particularly dangerous, for language shapes the way we experience the world. The Churches are ceasing to use language that is capable of taking hold of people and placing them in contact with our fundamental religious symbols. Liturgical committees seem ready to abandon the conotations and associations of liturgical forms that have developed over the centuries, simply because these forms are not 'in keeping' with today's standardised patterns of speech. A healthy Church will reverse this trend.

As I was researching part of this chapter the Swiss-German theologian Hans Küng visited Britain. He confirmed David Martin's observation that many are looking *outside* the Churches, even for religious belief. 'They find,' he says, 'too big a difference between the Churches and Jesus Christ himself.' So they conclude that they are for Jesus but not for Churches. In short, Küng asserts, the Christian churches have to become more Christian. By looking more closely at Jesus himself the Churches could change many of their attitudes considerably. Then, says Küng, 'we would be, for instance, more understanding in the question of birth-control; we would be more pitiful in the question of divorce; we would be more active in the questions of ecumenism; and I think we would be a little more democratic and equal before God in our churches.'

Hans Küng thinks this can happen. As a Roman Catholic he remains extremely critical of the way his own Church as well as other Churches operates at present. His 700-page book *On being a Christian* includes a programme of revolution for those who want to change the Churches from the bottom upwards. '*One member of the parish who goes to the parish priest does not count,*' he writes, '*five can be troublesome, fifty can change the situation. One parish priest does not count in the diocese, five are given attention, fifty are invincible.*'[13]

Now even if all these changes begin to take place – if we sell off our redundant churches, pay the clergy properly, allow the laity to be the Church, demolish our unrepresentative and bureaucratic structures, begin to love and learn more from other denominations, and recover some of the real roots of our religion – there is no certainty that more people will be brought into Church. We might well lose people. We shall lose those laity who want to leave everything to the clergy. We shall lose those clergy who cannot bear not to dominate everything. But in that case a leaner Church will be a healthier one. And in any case our calling is above all else to seek the Kingdom of God.[14] It is God's responsibility whether or not the churches are filled as a result.

I am not, therefore, offering a recipe for filling churches with new people. By changing the structures of the Churches we do not automatically change those structures of the world that are at present hostile to Christianity. Bryan Wilson believes that in today's society we meet each other not so much as individual persons or whole beings but rather as 'role players'. We meet people mostly in their capacity as technicians or bureaucrats or civil servants or whatever it might be. We live in a much more ordered and rationally structured world of this kind than we did in the past, and our relationships are much more impersonal. In consequence, says Bryan Wilson, we no longer need the interpretations of social relationships that the churches offered us in the past. 'And what the Churches have to say about trust, about faith, about good behaviour, about decency, and so on, appears to be less and less the determining features of our relationships. These relationships are now determined by strictly technical rules.'

Although Christians may deplore such impoverished relationships and feel helpless to change them the situation will not last for ever. Society changes. For instance, we have already identified those at the lowest end of the working class (sociologically) as belonging to a group that stopped going to church in the nineteenth century partly because their low assessment of themselves and the value of their work made them feel they possessed little to offer God or thank him for. The Revd Brian Cordingley draws attention to many elements in our society that are now making such people feel more significant and responsible. He instances the 'social contract', the increasing awareness that if we are to have a good nation, workers must be consulted and taken seriously. Workers have a status today unique in Britain since the industrial revolution. Inevitably this will have a profound effect on people's consciousness. Brian Cordingley thinks there may well be a need on the part of working people to ask some new questions about where they are going, about what life is all about and what they want from it. So, he says, there may be opportunities sooner than we think for the gospel to become very obviously meaningful to them.

The effect on Christianity might be equally profound. Max Weber observed of people whose lives are spent 'at the lower end of, or altogether outside of, the social hierarchy,' that 'Since these groups are not bound by the social conventions, they are capable of an original attitude toward the meaning of the cosmos, and since they are not impeded by any material considerations, they are capable of intense ethical and religious sentiment.'[15]

Will the Churches in Britain be capable of responding to this intense ethical and religious sentiment? In the meantime they have far more to do than just wait and see. For one thing, the Churches will not remotely be able to answer these new questions analysed by Brian Cordingley unless they start learning what the world is like for those who never look inside our church buildings. In researching this book I was repeatedly told that most of what the Churches have to say is completely irrelevant to the important issues in people's lives today. Inside the Churches we must learn to listen to those few lay men and women left to us who lead their lives immersed in the real world outside. We must use our industrial chaplains, our hospital chaplains, our army chaplains, our school chaplains, to feed back into the Churches' thinking what they have discovered in the world, before we can even begin to think what the gospel might have to say about, for example, industrial democracy or piece-work or wage differentials, or redundancy, or wild-cat strikes. The world in which those things occur is at present impossibly remote from the introverted world of most of our Churches.[16]

In Norwich the Revd Jack Burton has been living in that world as, he says, 'a prophetic demonstration against modern, middle-class, out-of-touch Christianity.'[17] He confesses his disappointment that he has made not a single convert to church-going, for when he first started his experimental new ministry he thought he might. 'I thought that if I was near people,' he reflects, 'they couldn't fail to see the good sense of the gospel and respond wholeheartedly. How naive I was!'

One experimental ministry will not change the Churches, let alone overcome a century of alienation among working men and women. But instead of converts Jack Burton has brought to the Churches something probably more valuable at this moment: insight, about ourselves and about the world outside. He has learnt, he says, 'how curiously quaint the Church looks from outside,' and that the church-going habit will not suddenly re-emerge as so many hope and pray it will.

He has confronted far greater ignorance about the Bible than he imagined existed among ordinary people. He has discovered nonetheless how people value what he calls 'the folk-religion occasions, the funerals and the weddings and the christenings.' He has learnt that those apparently indifferent to a lot of religion do respond to friendship, warmth, sympathy, acceptance and patience. For him now two of the most important words are, he says, 'presence' and 'unity'.

Jack Burton's ministry has not only shown that there are no slick answers to the Churches' problems; it also brings into prominence the question raised by any kind of 'auxiliary ministry': what is the fundamental reason for an ordained professional ministry? According to the New Testament *all* Christians constitute 'a royal priesthood.'[18] In the course of Christian history this basic truth has sometimes faded almost into oblivion. The increasing separation of the clerical order from the laity led the Churches to forget the fact that every Christian possesses a priesthood and that even though some may be specially commissioned to lead Christian worship, preach to the Christian community and pronounce God's forgiveness, all Christians are called to evangelize, proclaim the redemption of the world and offer worship for that redemption.

As a result, Bishop F. R. Barry once wrote, if a press photographer wanted to take a picture of the Churches at work he would certainly look for a scene in which parsons were prominently doing something. But, asked Bishop Barry, 'is that the kind of picture it ought to be, or ought it not to be something quite different— a class room perhaps, or a council home, or a factory?'[19] Until the Churches properly grapple with these questions they will not be ready to receive new lay support. They will continue to deploy lay men and women chiefly to raise money, run clubs and trim churchyards, activities not without value but which deflect our minds from the fact that God not only created the whole world of art and science and technology, but also calls us to co-operate in its redemption.

Since clerical domination is an integral part of this problem, it is absurd to expect the clergy to transform the churches at this point. I repeat Jimmy Hamilton-Brown's conviction that 'we have to have far fewer clergy and far more laity actually doing things and saying things and being leaders in the church.' He further sees that in such a situation many clergymen will feel lost, especially where a working-class pattern of lay leadership is emerging.[20] 'If I had to work in a working-class parish,' he admits, 'I honestly wouldn't know where to start.'

Although Jimmy Hamilton-Brown is aware of Christians in all our major conurbations who are trying to cope with the problems raised by such areas, he points to Manchester in particular as a place where some answers are being found. There, he says, Christians are discovering that they must work in small groups, to study the Bible and pray and talk and think. And not all people in these groups need be Christians, he maintains; the groups should be open to anyone.

In Manchester too, at work in the area called Moss Side, I met a man who has achieved remarkable results in Christian service and commitment to the world. The Revd Gerry Wheale went as an Anglican rector to Moss side in 1962 and found the local authority about to demolish half the houses in his parish. Since this proposal was the main concern of everyone living there, Gerry Wheale himself became involved in it. At first he simply tried to help those who had been displaced by the demolition activities of what he calls a 'rather insensitive' local authority. Then he, and a group of people gathered round him, decided to go further and start their own Housing Association: Moss Care.

By this time he had come to rely increasingly on Christians of all denominations in Moss Side, through the local Council of Churches. He describes how a group from this Council of Churches, sitting in his old church hall, decided they could not simply sit in judgement on the local authority without also trying to make a contribution of their own to solving the housing problem (and thus coming to understand better some of the problems facing the local authority). A dozen people sitting in that church has subscribed £50 each. The Mothers' Union in Manchester gave them £1,200. Ten years later the Housing

Association set up with this money owned in the region of 400 properties and had on hand a £200 million programme of rehabilitation.

Apart from Gerry Wheale's parish hall for its offices. Moss Care draws no resources from the institutional Churches. It employs four community officers of its own. It is a Christian ecumenical project that lives off the land, surviving and flourishing in the kind of area that many Churches have pulled out of.

Gerry Wheale sees his commission as a parish priest in that place to be involved in this work. But, taking his laity seriously, he has had many detailed conversations with his Parochial Church Council as to whether or not this work can be understood as a legitimate part of a parish priest's ministry. 'This,' he says, 'is the business of participation in church circles, as far as I'm concerned.'

Gerry Wheale's work is far removed from what we usually expect the Churches to be doing. Yet it embodies very many of the elements vital for Churches that want to become healthy again. He would like to think that he has found a pattern for the Churches' ministry in the future. He spreads some of his ideas as a tutor on the North West Ordination Course. But he says, 'I'm not sure that the Church has got the imagination or – let me use another word – the faith to commit itself to the world in the way that we have done.'

At that one point I think Gerry Wheale may be wrong. In this investigation of the health of the British Churches I have heard the death-rattle in much of the old institutions. But I have also discovered many points of hope: a new understanding of the importance of the laity; a number of clergymen who are deeply immersed in the problems and hopes of the real world; a rediscovery among some Christians of the natural and deep roots of our religion; a willingness here and there to learn from other Christian traditions; new and exciting forms of experimental ministry, as the Churches begin to realise that the old ways no longer always work; an understanding of those aspects of twentieth-century British society we can control and change,

along with an acceptance of those we simply have to live with;
and the possibility of smaller, leaner and yet healthier
Churches, aware that what ultimately matters is not their own
survival. What matters is unconditional commitment to seek
and serve the Kingdom of God. This may involve the death of
much that we have relied on in the past. But it will be dying to
live again.

1. Michael Hill *A Sociology of Religion*, Heinemann 1973, p. 249.
2. The address of the Christian Education Movement is 2 Chester House,
    Pages Lane, London N10 1PR.
3. The address of the Institute of Religion and Medicine is St Mary
    Abchurch Vestry, Abchurch Lane, London E.C.4.
4. E.g. the symposium *Religion and Medicine 2*, ed. M. H. Melinsky, S.C.M.
    Press 1973.
5. Its address is Church House, Dean's Yard, London SW1P 3NZ.
6. The address of Christian Aid is P.O. Box No. 1, London SW9 8BH.
7. Janet Lacey *A Cup of Water: the Story of Christian Aid*, Hodder and
    Stoughton 1970, pp. 35, 33 and 101.
8. *Resources: the Committee of Forty Report*, Blackwood and Sons, Edinburgh
    1975, p. 1; *Report of the Committee of Forty*, Blackwood and Sons, Edinburgh
    1976, pp. 10–15.
9. *Community Parishes and Small Groups*, ed. Norman Swan, Edinburgh n.d.
    p. 13.
10. N. Pevsner and D. Lloyd *Hampshire and the Isle of Wight*, Penguin books
    1967, p. 694.
11. Information from the British Council and Churches Division of
    Ecumenical Affairs Digest of the Register of Local Ecumenical Projects,
    January 1977.
12. This is the theme of Ernst Lange *Die ökumenische Utopie*, Kreuz Verlag,
    Stuttgart 1972, which is written in the form of letters to a Marxist (and
    urgently demands translation).
13. H. Küng *On Being a Christian*, tr. Edward Quinn, Collins 1977, p. 528.
14. Matthew 6.33; Luke 12.31.
15. M. Weber *Economy and Society*, p. 507.
16. Two examples of this rare kind of Christian thinking are Brian
    Cordingley's essay 'Strikes as seen by an industrial chaplain,' in
    Perspectives on Strikes, ed. R. H. Preston, S.C.M. Press 1975, and Michael
    Wilson *Health is for People*, Darton, Longman and Todd 1975.
17. J. Burton *Transport of Delight*, S.C.M. Press 1976, p. 17.

18. I Peter 2.9.
19. F. R. Barry 'The case for part time priests,' in *Part-time Priests?*, ed. Robin Denniston, Skeffington 1960, p. 12.
20. On this pattern see David Sheppard *Built as a City*. pp. 285–98.

Some Books

Tracts against the Times by David Martin (Lutterworth Press 1974), especially Chapter 14, 'Can the Church survive?', is an excellent antidote to excessive gloom in the face of secularisation. David Martin writes (p. 14) that, 'there is a double question mark: the survival of the Church and the survival of secularity. I desire both.'

An antidote to excessive confidence is *Built as a City: God and the Urban World Today* (Hodder and Stoughton 1974), written by David Sheppard when he was Bishop of Woolwich, in the belief (p. 11) that 'The Church's life in big cities has been marked by its inability to establish a strong, locally rooted Christian presence among the groups that society leaves without voice or power.'

Among the books I have quoted in these pages the nearest to a masterpiece is Hanns Küng's *On being a Christian* (S.C.M. Press 1977). It is, however, extremely long (though not so long as the author intended: see pages 686f., n.80) and perhaps best read in sections rather than at one sitting. Especially relevant to *Cry God for England* are pp. 517 to 529: 'Criticism of the Church', 'Why stay?', 'Practical suggestions', 'Against discouragement', and 'Why can we hope?'. Küng recapitulates (p. 602) his overall aim in writing *On being a Christian* as to demonstrate that,

> *By following Jesus Christ*
> *man in the world of today*
> *can truly humanly live, act, suffer and die:*
> *in happiness and unhappiness, life and death,*
> *sustained by God and helpful to men.*

In *The Pentecostals* (S.C.M. Press 1969) Walter J. Hollenweger is as prolix as Hans Küng. But his informative, well-documented and thoroughly objective book is essential reading for those who wish to understand the background to a growing group of Christians whose practices are still strange to many in Britain.

A Question of Conscience by Charles Davis (Hodder and Stoughton 1967) movingly and painfully takes stock of his position as a Christian after leaving the institutional Church. Part III is called 'Prospect for the Church'. Easier to read but ultimately less rewarding is Nick Stacey's autobiographical *Who Cares?* (Anthony Blond 1971).

No major book about industrial mission or new forms of ministry has yet been written. E. R. Wickham's *Church and People in an Industrial City* (Lutterworth Press 1957) is resolutely historical and confines itself to the city of Sheffield, apart from the last chapter, 'The Mission of the Church in an industrial society', which is still worth reading, though written when British industrial mission was in its infancy. *Priest and Worker: the autobiography of Henri Perrin*, translated by Bernard Wall (Macmillan 1965) gives insight into the inspiration behind similar movements in France – and also indicates the stress the institutional Churches can cause in pioneers.

Altogether remarkable is Jack Burton's *Transport of Delight* (S.C.M. Press 1976), outlining in diary form a year in his life as a minister and bus driver. Preaching on Sundays, slipping into Norwich Cathedral for evensong whenever his shift allows it, Jack Burton reveals a developed Christian spirituality renewed by contact with the world.

Although *Cry God for England* is not about the intellectual credibility of Christianity, it does raise fundamental questions about the interpretation of the Bible. Those who are not starting from scratch and have strong stomachs could read D. E. Nineham's introduction (pp. 15 to 52) to his commentary on *The Gospel of St Mark* (Penguin Books 1963). *Redating the New Testament* by John A. T. Robinson (S.C.M. Press 1976) may seem concerned with a limited subject; but as the author observes (p. 358), 'dates remain disturbingly fundamental data.' This book should really be read in its entirety, though its most important chapters are I, 'Dates and Data', and XI, 'Conclusions and corollaries'. 'My position,' Robinson writes (p. 11), 'will probably seem surprisingly conservative – especially to those who judge me radical on other issues.' What surprises him is the slender evidence supporting many generally accepted assumptions of New Testament scholarship.

Those who wish to discover how a rigorous theologian can still find the New Testament inspiring should not miss Helmut Thielicke's short book *How Modern Should Theology Be?* (Fontana 1970), especially chapter 3, 'Understanding the Miracle Stories'. But no reading about the Bible is a substitute for reading the Bible itself.

Finally, to those who wish to look at the historical background of the present state of the Established Church I cannot recommend too highly the witty and scholarly revised version of *Leaders of the Church of England, 1828–1978*, by David L. Edwards (Hodder and Stoughton 1978).

Who's Who

Colin Barnett is a regional secretary of the T.U.C. and North West Divisional Officer of the National Union of Public Employees. For two years he worked as an administrative assistant to the Revd Lord Soper. He has been connected with the Churches' industrial mission for 25 years. He describes himself as coming out of the Christian Socialist tradition and standing left-of-centre.

After working for three years as a curate in Cheadle, Cheshire, the Revd Colin O. Buchanan moved to St John's Theological College, Nottingham, where he has been successively tutor, registrar, director of studies and Vice-Principal. In 1970 he was elected a proctor on the Church of England's York Convocation.

The Revd Jack Burton is a Methodist minister who earns his living driving a bus in Norwich. He published *Transport of Delight* (S.C.M. Press) in 1976.

The Rev Brian L. Cordingley was ordained in 1957 as an industrial missioner in the Anglican Diocese of Sheffield. In 1963 he moved to Manchester as senior industrial missioner in the Diocese of Manchester. He took a six months' sabbatical in 1976 to study Catholic and Protestant industrial mission in Europe, and the following year was appointed Manchester Diocesan Development Officer for Urban and Industrial Mission. His work as secretary of the British Industrial Mission Association repeatedly takes him abroad, especially to the E.E.C. countries.

The Revd Fr CHARLES DAVIS, who resigned in 1966 after 20 years as a Roman Catholic priest and theologian, is now professor of religion at Concordia University, Montreal.

The Most Revd GEORGE PATRICK DWYER, born in 1908, was educated at Cambridge and the English College in Rome. After teaching and editing Roman Catholic journals he became Bishop of Leeds and then in 1965 Archbishop of Birmingham.

The Revd J. L. M. FARMBOROUGH worked as a curate in Wolverhampton and London before spending six years as chaplain at All Saints', Niteroi, Brazil, and another five years as organising secretary of the South American Missionary Society. In 1970 he became Vicar of Marple, Cheshire.

The Revd JAMES J. HAMILTON-BROWN holds a B.Sc. of the University of London. In 1975, after eight years as Vicar of Bramcote, he was appointed Research and Development Officer of the Archbishop of Canterbury's Council on Evangelism.

As well as running a Methodist Church in Cheshire the Revd Dr BERNARD E. JONES is a secretary of the Church Membership Committee of the Methodist Church Division of Ministries.

Mrs UNA KROLL, who is qualified in medicine and surgery, works as a deaconess at the Anglican church of St Peter, Morden, in the Diocese of Southwark.

HANS KÜNG who is professor of dogmatic and ecumenical theology and director of the institute of ecumenical studies at the University of Tübingen, remains remarkably pacific and prolific despite what he calls 'the tiresome disputes' forced on him by Rome (*On being a Christian*, p. 686). He dedicated his book *The Church* (tr. Ray and Rosaleen Ockenden, Burns and Oates 1967) to Dr Michael Ramsey, the former Archbishop of Canterbury.

DAVID MARTIN has taught at the London School of Economics since 1962, first as lecturer, then as reader and lastly (since 1971) as professor of sociology. He writes on theology and religion as well as sociology, and his published works include *Patterns of Secularisation* (Routledge and Kegan Paul 1969) and *Tracts against the Times* (Lutterworth Press 1974).

Dr STUART MEWS is a Methodist layman who teaches sociology in the department of religious studies at the University of Lancaster.

The Revd Dr COLIN MORRIS was born in Bolton, Lancashire, in 1929, and after attending the local county grammar school was educated at the Universities of Oxford and Manchester. After ordination he worked as a Methodist missionary in Northern Rhodesia from 1956 to 1960. He then spent four years as president of the United Church of Central Africa and a further three years as president of the United Church of Zambia. From 1973 to 1978 he was general secretary of the Methodist Missionary Society. He now works for the B.B.C. as Head of Religious Broadcasting, Television.

The Revd ROBIN E. NIXON after ordination was first an Anglican curate and then tutor at Cranmer Hall, Durham. For 12 years he was senior tutor at St John's Theological College, Durham, before becoming principal of St John's Theological College, Nottingham. He has edited *The Churchman* since 1972.

The Revd Dr EDWARD NORMAN, who has been Dean of Peterhouse College, Cambridge, since 1971, has also been a schoolmaster as well as a fellow of several other Cambridge Colleges. In 1965 he was made a Fellow of the Royal Historical Society. Oxford University Press published his *Church and Society in England* in 1976.

The Rt Revd Dr JOHN A. T. ROBINSON, Dean of Trinity College, Cambridge, since 1969, became famous as Bishop of

Woolwich when he wrote *Honest to God* (Penguin Books 1963). Before that time he had been a curate to Mervyn Stockwood in Bristol, Dean of Clare College, Cambridge, and lecturer in divinity in the University.

The Rt Revd PATRICK CAMPBELL RODGER became Bishop of Oxford in 1978, after eight years as Bishop of Manchester. Before that he had been a chaplain to university students, S.C.M. secretary for Great Britain and Ireland, provost of St Mary's Cathedral, Edinburgh, and executive secretary of the Faith and Order Council of the World Council of Churches. In 1974 he was appointed chairman of the Churches' Unity Commission for England.

The Revd Dr ANDREW ROSS, who has worked as a Church of Scotland missionary in Africa, is now senior lecturer in the department of ecclesiastical history at the University of Edinburgh.

The Rt Revd DAVID S. SHEPPARD, Bishop of Liverpool since 1975, has played cricket for Cambridge (captain 1952), captained Sussex and played 22 times for England (captain 1954). He worked as an Anglican curate in Islington and then ran the Mayflower Family Centre in Canning Town, before being consecrated Bishop of Woolwich.

Before ordination into the Anglican ministry the Revd NICOLAS D. STACEY served in the Royal Navy as a midshipman and sub-lieutenant. As an international sprinter he took part in the British Empire Games in 1949 and the Olympic Games in 1952 (semi-finalist in the 200 metres; finalist in the 4 × 400 metres relay). He was domestic chaplain to the Bishop of Birmingham and then worked as a parish priest in London from 1960 to 1968, before becoming successively deputy-director of OXFAM, Director of Social Services for the London Borough of Ealing and Director of Social Services for Kent County Council.

The Rt Revd Dr MERVYN STOCKWOOD, Bishop of Southwark since 1959, worked as a Vicar in Bristol from 1922 to 1955 (where he became a Labour councillor) and then ran the University Church in Cambridge.

The Revd Fr SIMON TUGWELL was educated at Lancing and Oxford. Converted to the Roman Catholic Church, he was admitted as a Dominican in 1965 and ordained priest in 1971.

JILL TWEEDIE, a freelance journalist and regular contributor to *The Guardian*, for two years ran a programme for women on Thames TV. She is writing a book on love.

The Revd G. A. WHEALE holds the degree of M.Ed. He has worked as a clergyman in Lagos as well as in this country. He is associated with the William Temple Foundation, in the Manchester Business School, and teaches on the North West Ordination Course.

The Most Revd DEREK WORLOCK, who was born in London in 1920, was ordained in 1944, consecrated a bishop in 1965, and in 1976 became Roman Catholic Archbishop of Liverpool.

Among the numerous published writings of Dr BRYAN R. WILSON, reader in sociology at Oxford since 1962, are *Religious Sects* (Penguin Books 1970) and *Contemporary Transformations of Religious Consciousness* (Oxford University Press 1976). In 1971 he became president of the Conférence Internationale de Sociologie Réligieuse.